P9-CDN-062

JOHN L. STODDARD'S LECTURES

SCOTLAND ENGLAND

LONDON

Norwood Press
J. S. Cushing & Co. — Berwick & Smith
Norwood, Mass., U.S.A.

Macdonald & Sons, Bookbinders, Boston

SWAN ISLAND, LOCH LOMOND.

JOHN L. STODDARD'S LECTURES

COMPLETE IN TEN VOLUMES

VOLUME NINE

BOSTON
BALCH BROTHERS CO.
MCMVII
CHICAGO: GEO. L. SHUMAN & CO.

SCOTLAND

A HIGHLAND COTTAGE.

IN Scotland Heroism and Romance go hand in hand. Its Heroism is like a mediæval castle, still haughtily defiant of the wintry storms. Its Romance is the ivy, which covers the historic ruin with a mantle of protection, caresses it with countless clinging fingers, and tenderly conceals the ravages of Time and man. Scotland, although one of the smallest of European countries, has, nevertheless, produced a galaxy of heroes, whose names are still the synonyms of daring and of chivalry. Moreover, since heroic deeds invariably call forth men to guard their memory by song and story, the land of Bruce and Wallace has, also, been the home of Robert Burns and the immortal novelist of Abbotsford.

LOCH ACHRAY AND BEN VENUE.

As for the element of sentiment, aside from all that Scott has given us in prose and poetry, one beautiful romantic life illumines Scotland's history, like the long, golden twilight of its northern summer; for Mary, Queen of Scots, is one of the most fascinating and mysterious of female characters. More volumes have been written in regard to her than about any other woman in the world. Of her transcendent beauty, and, alas! her suffering, there is no question; but how far she deserved her tragic fate has always been a theme of bitter controversy. Such is the mystery which enshrouds her life that she has been well called the "Enigma of History." By some, she has been painted as an angel of goodness; by others, branded as the worst of criminals. The truth lies, probably, between the two extremes. National hate, religious prejudice, and the base treachery of her nobles combined, no doubt, to ruin her and then to cover up the crime with slander. This would hardly have been possible had not her life given some occasion for such accusations; but, even at the worst, a multitude of lovely and heroic traits so powerfully plead for her, that thousands, year by year, still read the story of her life with breathless interest, and view it through a mist of tears.

MARY, QUEEN OF SCOTS.

One of the most delightful routes by which to enter

BALMORAL CASTLE, THE HIGHLAND HOME OF THE QUEEN.

Scotland is the river Clyde. The shipyards of the Clyde! Who has not heard of them? Whole navies there are seen in embryo. For miles the river's banks are lined with half-built steamers, which look like skeletons of prehistoric monsters of the sea suspended in mid air. Who would suppose,

SHIPPING ON THE CLYDE.

SHIPBUILDING ON THE CLYDE.

in looking at their uncouth forms, that they could ever be developed into the marvelous specimens of strength and beauty, which we subsequently see riding the waves, as if instinct with life, conveying thousands every year with speed and safety from the Old World to the New, and bearing on their storm-defying prows such names as the Campania and Lucania? Yet, close beside the river, a few years ago, when excavations were being made to enlarge the harbor of

DUMBARTON CASTLE.

Glasgow, an ancient boat of solid oak was found, not planked or built, but hewn from the trunk of a stalwart tree. Within it lay an ax-head of laboriously sharpened stone, proving that boats were made by savages along the Clyde, ages ago, when neither iron nor bronze was known, but when the inhabitants of Scotland were still in the Stone Period of their evolution. What a prodigious, almost inconceivable, development of intellect is illustrated by a comparison between that tree-trunk of the Clyde, hollowed by fire and a rough stone ax, and the magnificent "ocean greyhounds," built there now, propelled by steam, managed by intricate machinery, lighted by electricity, and guided by the magnetic needle!

WALLACE STATUE, ABERDEEN.

A very different feature of the Clyde is the stern, formidable mountain called "Dumbarton Rock." Its form reminds one of the "Castled crag of Drachenfels" frowning above the river Rhine; but this old hill of Scotland has a history far more impressive than that of its German rival. The Drachenfels boasts only of a legendary dragon slain upon its cliffs, but old Dumbarton calls to mind the human hero — William Wallace — since it was by the commander of this fortress, six hundred years ago, that the mightiest and most daring of all Scotland's chieftains was shamefully betrayed to his enemies.

Despite the centuries which have since elapsed, the world has not forgotten Wallace. Even this almost impregnable rock was not considered secure enough to hold him. Accordingly he was conveyed to London. Crowds gathered there to see him pass, and gazed with awe on the renowned and dreaded prisoner. Meantime the King of England thirsted for his blood. The thirst was quickly slaked; for, after a mock trial in London, the gallant Wallace was condemned to die. What a death was that reserved for him! He was first hanged, but cut down while alive; then, portions of his body were torn out and burned before his face; and, finally, after atrocious sufferings, his head was struck off by the executioner and placed upon a pole on London Bridge. Even then his body was dismembered. His right arm was

WALLACE STATUE, ON THE WALLACE MONUMENT.

displayed at Newcastle; his left at Berwick; one leg was sent to Perth; the other to the town of Aberdeen: yet England's triumph was of short duration.

Above a densely wooded hill near Stirling, where Wallace had, some years before, defeated England's army of invasion, rises a massive monument of stone two hundred and twenty feet in height. It is the National Memorial to Wallace. It stands as he stood, solitary, unshaken, and majestic, towering above

A DISTANT VIEW OF THE WALLACE MONUMENT.

the country he so gallantly defended. It is a striking illustration of the fact that to destroy a man like Wallace is impossible. Burn, cut, or crucify the body if you will, if he who dies thus stands for some immortal truth, his soul emerges from the mutilated casket indestructible, and travels triumphant down the path of history.

"Speak, History! Who are life's victors? Unroll thy long annals and say:
Are they those whom the world called victors, who won the success of a day?
The martyrs, or Nero? The Spartans who fell at Thermopylæ's tryst,
Or the Persians and Xerxes? His judges, or Socrates? Pilate, or Christ?"

Rivaling, in point of interest and numbers, the statues of Wallace in Scotland are those of his successor, — Robert Bruce. Only a brief interval occurred between these heroes; for, goaded into fury by the cruel murder of her champion, within six months after the death of Wallace, Scotland had risen again and had proclaimed the gallant Bruce her king. A complete record of his exploits would fill many pages. A hundred episodes in his career could give material for an epic poem. The story of his struggles for Scotland's freedom forms a northern Iliad, and Homer would have been proud to sing of him as of Achilles. Homeless and penniless, hunted by England, excommunicated by the Pope, he, nevertheless, fought desperately on, until the object of his life was reached and not a particle of Scottish heather was crushed beneath an English foot. To those who love the memory of Bruce, no spot in

THE WALLACE MONUMENT.

THE STATUE OF ROBERT BRUCE.

FLAGSTAFF STONE, BANNOCKBURN.

Scotland is more interesting than the scene of his most glorious victory,— Bannockburn. Nearly six hundred years have come and gone since that eventful day, yet one may still see here the very stone in which the Scottish standard was then placed, just as a modern flagstaff rises close beside it now. Bannockburn is the Marathon of Scotland. The English army numbered one hundred thousand men; the Scots had less than forty thousand; but they were fighting for their fatherland, and they were led by Robert Bruce.

THE FIELD OF BANNOCKBURN.

Before the battle Bruce had caused innumerable holes and trenches to be dug here, which after-

BEN NEVIS AND RUINS OF INVERLOCHY CASTLE.

ward were carefully concealed with turf. Accordingly the field, which looked to the enemy firm and undisturbed, was, in reality, a death-trap for the English cavalry. As the invading host advanced, the Scots knelt down and solemnly invoked the aid of God. "What are they doing," cried the English king, "kneeling already for our mercy?" He was soon undeceived; for, rising from their knees, the Scots attacked their foes, not, as in modern times, from a distance with artillery, but hand to hand with sword and battle-ax, until the English were completely vanquished and fled in wild disorder from the field.

Upon the plain near Stirling I noted with great interest a carefully preserved memorial of the past, in the form of a dark, weather-beaten stone, placed upon a pedestal and guarded by an iron screen. On this all traitors to the cause of Scotland were beheaded. A gruesome object lesson truly; but, after all, the Scots do well to keep such monuments as these. Who has not seen a Scotchman's blue eyes kindle when his native land was mentioned? It is not strange, for Scotchmen lead their children to these landmarks of their country's history, and under the same sky that Robert Bruce beheld, and in the shadow of the Wallace monument, repeat to them those deeds which are their nation's proudest heritage.

DECAPITATION STONE, NEAR STIRLING.

Scotland is so diminutive that it is easy to turn in a few hours from these scenes of warlike memories to a more peaceful section of old Scotland, the quiet, little town of Ayr, rich in its souvenirs of Robert Burns. "More hero-worship," does one say? Ah! but believe me, the time is never wasted which we spend in honoring departed greatness. The trouble with this age is, not too much respect and reverence, but too little. Great men are like great mountains: they lift our thoughts above the ordinary level of humanity; they give us hope and inspiration. In studying the heroes of the past we, too, are stimulated to heroic deeds; and when we read the biographies of men of genius, — from Plutarch's Lives to those of Washington and Lincoln, — we draw instinctively a deeper breath, as when upon a sultry day there suddenly is brought to us the cool, exhilarating freshness of the sea. Before in-

HIGH STREET. AYR.

THE "TWA BRIGS."

A HIGHLAND COTTAGE.

vestigating the subject, I had no idea how many people go to Ayr to render homage to the poet's memory. They number, on an average, more than thirty thousand, annually. I know of nothing like this in the world. Even the pilgrims to the home of Shakespeare do not exceed fourteen thousand, yearly. It shows how deeply and imperishably Burns is enshrined in the affections of the English-speaking race, in spite of the difficulty to many readers of understanding his Scotch dialect. The town

"THE AULD BRIG O' DOON," AYR.

abounds in quaint reminders of the poet who has given it such fame. Thus, the Old Bridge of Ayr is very little changed since the time of Burns, and casts its shadow in the stream below just as it did when the inspired plowman used to lean upon its time-worn parapet. In his day, however, a New Bridge had been erected a little farther down the stream, and Burns describes the fancied rivalry between them. Standing upon the "Auld Brig," as it is called, one recollects how the New Bridge is made to say to it, disdainfully,

"Will your poor, narrow foot-path of a street,
Where twa wheelbarrows tremble when they meet,
Your ruin'd, formless bulk o' stane and lime,
Compare wi' bonie brigs o' modern time ?"

to which the ancient structure answers proudly,

"I'll be a brig, when ye're a shapeless cairn."

Strangely enough, the poet's prophecy proved true. The venerable arches, built six hundred years ago, are still in use, while the New Bridge, constructed only a century since, has been superseded already by a newer one.

ALLOWAY KIRK, AYR.

A short walk from the hotel in Ayr brought us to Alloway's witch-haunted kirk. It is a picturesque old ruin, in the tower of which still hangs the ancient bell which is regarded by the peasants with superstitious reverence. But even when standing in the graveyard of this church, beside the tombstone of William Burns, the poet's father, I could not feel in the least degree serious; for Burns has made this place forever humorous as the scene of Tam O'Shanter's ludicrous adventure on the night when

"a child might understand
The deil had business on his hand."

TAM O'SHANTER AND SOUTER JOHNNY.

One must be heavy-hearted, indeed, not to be amused as he recalls the mirth-provoking stanzas of that poem, while he beholds the very window through which the unearthly light streamed forth that lured the ill-fated Tam to peep at the uncanny sight of witches dancing in mad glee, while the Devil furnished the music on a bagpipe, and, sitting upright in their coffins, each corpse held a lighted candle in its hand. Tam O'Shanter was not an altogether fictitious character; for the original of Burns' hero was a certain Douglas Graham, of Shanter Farm not far away, and on his tombstone in the village churchyard he is designated, not only by his real, but also by his poetic title. Moreover one sees in Ayr, to-day, the "Tam O'Shanter Inn,"—the identical tavern where Tam caroused so long with his boon com-

THE "TAM O'SHANTER INN," AYR.

panion, Souter Johnny, and above the doorway is a rude painting portraying Tam and Johnny drinking bumpers to each other's health, and reminding one of the lines:

> "Kings may be blest, but Tam was glorious,
> O'er a' the ills o' life victorious!"

Not far away is the bridge across which the affrighted tippler rode for dear life on his gray mare, Maggie, believing that the evil spirits which, he thought, were after him would have no power to cross a running stream.

All visitors to Ayr drive about two miles from the town to the little cottage, so famous as the birthplace of the peasant poet. It needs but a glance at the low-roofed, humble room where Burns was born to convince us that he was essentially a man of the people. He is a splendid proof of the democracy of genius. Never was there a better illustration

THE BURNS COTTAGE, AND ROOM WHERE BURNS WAS BORN.

ALONG THE RIVER BANK.

of the truth that a poet is born, not made. His was a genuine inspiration. He said of himself that his passions raged like so many devils until they found vent in rhyme; yet his brother Gilbert declared that Robert never wrote half the brilliant thoughts that flowed from his lips while he was cutting peat in the bog. Burns did not claim to be a student. Scholarship is, of course, desirable; but poets do not always need scholastic training. Great scholars are too frequently as dry as the parchments they peruse. Bloodless as ghosts and passionless as dust, they never really touch humanity; but Robert Burns, with youth's warm blood coursing impetuously through his veins, frankly exclaims:

"Gie me a spark of Nature's fire!
That's a' the learning I desire.
Then, tho' I drudge thro' dub an' mire
At plow or cart,
My muse, — tho' hamely in attire, —
May touch the heart!"

That it did touch the heart, we are reminded when we leave

the house and stroll beside the neighboring stream which his sad verses have immortalized.

> "Ye banks and braes o' bonnie Doon, —
> How can ye bloom sae fresh and fair ?
> How can ye chant, ye little birds,
> And I sae weary, fu' o' care ?"

Who has not felt at times the cruel contrast between smiling nature and a breaking heart; and, feeling it, who has not found in Robert Burns a friend? For Burns, like Byron, speaks directly to the emotions; and it is through the emotions that we really live. Moreover Burns, like Byron, is at once intelligible. One of the most attractive features of his poetry, like that of all things truly great, is its simplicity. His stanzas need no teachers to expound their meaning. We find in them no mysteries to be debated by a class of students. The throbbings of his heart awake, immediately, answering pulsations in our own.

"YE BANKS AND BRAES O' BONNIE DOON."

A BIT OF SCOTCH SCENERY.

Thus, the whole essence of a hundred love-stories has been condensed by Burns into four simple lines:

> "Had we never loved sae kindly,
> Had we never loved sae blindly,
> Never met, or never parted,
> We had ne'er been broken-hearted."

When have the joys of friendship ever been more truthfully expressed than in the exquisite lines of "Auld Lang Syne"?

In contrast to these humble memories of Burns, I looked with curiosity at several fine estates belonging to the aristocracy of Ayr, and recollected that the poet never lived in such luxury. On the contrary, in view of all the honors heaped upon him now, we think with infinite compassion of the poverty which hounded him to the grave. How bitterly he felt it his own pathetic letters tell. But one thing in him I admire with all my soul,—his hate of patronage. The only luxury he craved was that of being free from the necessity of asking or

THE BURNS MONUMENT, EDINBURGH.

receiving favors. As he himself exclaims, he desired money,

> "Not for to hide it in a hedge:
> Not for a train attendant:
> But for the glorious privilege
> Of being independent."

What wonder, then, that animated thus by poverty and pride the sympathy of Burns, in both the French and American Revolutions, was with the cause of freedom? Once, at a dinner party, he refused to drink the health of the Prime Minister of England — William Pitt — but proposed, instead, that of George Washington. Everywhere he was the same uncompromising democrat. Thus, though he gained for a time the attention of the fashionable world at Edinburgh, he never lost his head in all the flattery that was offered him. He understood it perfectly. He saw the lords and ladies stare at him as if he were a curious animal, and knew that, though they liked his poetry, they looked upon him with disdain and, had it not been for his indisputable genius, would not have come in contact with him Yet, now the only reason that those lords and ladies live in history is that they entertained the plowman Burns. Who does not recollect his splendid outburst against class distinctions, when he cries:

"What though on hamely fare we dine,
Wear hoddin gray an' a' that;
Gie fools their silks and knaves their wine,
A Man's a Man for a' that!
. . . .
You see yon birkie ca'ed 'a lord,'
Wha struts an' stares an a' that?
Tho' hundreds worship at his word,
He's but a coof for a' that.
. . . .
His ribband, star an' a' that,
The man o' independent mind,
He looks an' laughs at a' that!
. . . .
The rank is but the guinea's stamp,
The Man's the gowd for a' that!"

THE BURNS MEMORIAL, AYR.

INTERIOR OF THE BURNS MEMORIAL, AYR.

Upon a lovely hillside, near the town of Ayr, stands the Burns Monument, cutting its graceful Grecian silhouette against the sky. Within it are some interesting relics of the poet, together with his bust and portrait. The face of Burns is, above all else, lovable; and Burns was loved, and loved in turn, not wisely always, but too well. His sorrows, also, caused him often to seek oblivion in drink; yet now that he lies cold in death, his glorious black eyes no longer scintillant with mirth or passion, those blemishes are far more readily forgiven than would have been the qualities of meanness, treachery, and hypocrisy. The former faults sometimes exist together with a noble soul; the latter, never.

BESIDE THE BROOK.

Filled with these thoughts I stood beside the little brook where Burns and his

INTERIOR OF THE BURNS MAUSOLEUM, DUMFRIES.

Highland Mary said farewell to each other, before she returned home to prepare for their wedding. According to the solemn custom of the country, the lovers, when exchanging their vows of everlasting faithfulness, stood beside a stream of running water, emblem of eternity, and, holding a Bible between them, pledged their love and loyalty forever. They never met again, however, for Mary died soon after at her home. The Bible which they held is now preserved in the Burns Monument, at Ayr, and on a faded page we see his autograph and, beneath it, a tress of Mary's hair.

A tender melancholy is awakened by the sight of the grave of this fair girl whom Burns loved as he loved no other woman in his life. In the centre of the monument, delicately sculptured in relief, are the figures of the lovers, clasping hands in that pathetic leave-taking, which was so quickly followed by another, wherein the poet's fingers were replaced by the cold hand of Death. Below them are the simple words: "Erected over the grave of Highland Mary." No other name is there inscribed; but none is needed, for "Highland Mary" is the title she will now bear to the end of time.

GRAVE OF HIGHLAND MARY.

A pilgrimage to the haunts of Burns would be incomplete without a visit to the miserable house, at Dumfries, where he died at the age of thirty-seven. He had been for a long time

ROBERT BURNS.

ill, and it was while he lay upon his death-bed that he composed, to please the servant-maid who had been kind to him, one of the sweetest of his poems, "Oh, wert thou in the cauld blast," which has been rendered still more beautiful by the music composed for it by Mendelssohn. At this time, also, Burns was miserably poor. The volume of poems, which Scotland now regards as the most precious of her treasures, had brought him only forty-five dollars. A day or two before his death a merchant, for a bill of five pounds, had threatened to put him in jail and to turn his wife and children into the street. Burns was extremely sensitive. The horror of the situation killed him. His last words were a malediction on the man who had written him that threatening letter. Oh, the pathos of it! Now, now that he is dead, he is admired and almost worshiped by his countrymen. Statues and monuments have been erected to his memory in every part of Scotland; but, alas! how much in this world seems to come too late! The greatest of

HOUSE WHERE BURNS DIED, DUMFRIES.

Scotch poets died, owing a trifling debt; and now the world owes him a debt that it can never pay.

From the birthplace of Burns, a journey of only a few hours brings the tourist into the very heart of Scotland, the region of the Scottish Lakes, — the country of the Trossachs. The special charm of this enchanted land is not alone its mountain scenery: its greatest fascination lies in the fact that both its

THE COUNTRY OF THE TROSSACHS.

history and legends have been endeared to the whole English-speaking race by the transcendent genius of one man. This is not only Scotland: it is *Scott's* land; and guide-books are not needed here, so much as a previous reading of the "Waverley Novels," and the soul-stirring cantos of "Marmion," and the "Lady of the Lake." It is impossible to overestimate our indebtedness to Sir Walter for making Scotland's history and beauties so well known. In traveling here, we reap what he has sown, and we absorb with speed and comfort what cost him years of labor to accomplish. It is a great mistake to sup-

THE TOURIST'S STEAMER,
LOCH LOMOND.

LOCH KATRINE.

pose that all of Scott's charming descriptions came without effort from his pen. They are as absolutely accurate as if he had been writing a guide-book. Did he make one of his characters gallop a certain distance in a single day? He had first galloped it himself to see if it could be done. Moreover he always carefully noted even the names of the flowers and trees about the scenes which he was to describe. When a friend once remarked that he should think the author's imagination would supply such trifles, Scott replied, "No imagination can long retain its freshness, which is not nourished by a constant and minute study of Nature." In this connection, too, we may recall Byron's observation, that easy writing makes hard reading.

There is, perhaps, no better instance of a place in which poetical associations are more charmingly and inseparably blended with natural beauty than Loch Katrine. It is, indeed, diminutive, but through the genius of the "Great Magician" its fame has filled the world. It is a proof that Nature always needs the human element, even though it be fictitious, to permanently hold our interest. Without Scott's magic touch of poetry, this lake would be what scores of others in the world still are to us, — merely a placid mirror to reflect the blue of Heaven, but with no background of romantic history. Along the shore still curves the smooth white beach which, from its fair expanse of snow-white pebbles, bears the name that Scott bestowed upon it, — "The Silver Strand." This, as every reader of the poem knows, was the meeting-place of Fitz James, who had lost his way, and Ellen, "Lady of the Lake"; for, as the former blew a bugle blast to call, if possible, his scattered followers to his side,

THE SILVER STRAND, LOCH KATRINE.

"When lo! forth starting at the sound,
From underneath an agèd oak
That slanted from the islet rock,
A damsel guider of its way, . . .
A little skiff shot to the bay.
The boat had touch'd the silver strand,
Just as the hunter left his stand
And stood conceal'd amid the brake
To view this Lady of the Lake."

THE LADY OF THE LAKE.

It was a lovely summer morning, many years ago, that I first approached this heroine's wave-encircled home, still known as Ellen's Isle. On that occasion, my boat was rowed, not by a Highland lassie, to remind me of Scott's fair creation, but by a boatman rough, yet kind-hearted as a Scotch collie. In a peculiar dialect, half English and half Gaelic, he spoke of the places mentioned in the poem, as if they were historic sites. Nor is this strange. Immediately after the first edition of the "Lady of the Lake" appeared, crowds came to view the scenery of Loch Katrine, which, until then, had been comparatively unknown; and the subsequent summer (that of 1810) the public and private houses of the neighborhood were filled to overflowing with tourists. The stage-coach business, also, gained at once extraordinary activity and has been steadily increasing ever since. Truly, Napoleon was right when he exclaimed,

THE LANDING.

"Imagination rules the world." Never shall I forget that bright June morning on Loch Katrine. Save for the boatman, I was quite alone — the only denizen of the sylvan paradise where "Ellen" had once reigned supreme. The mountain breeze which broke into a thousand dimples the smiling surface of the lake, the songs of the awakened birds, the aromatic fragrance of the pines, and, finally, a

ELLEN'S ISLE.

charming sense of the absolute possession of a tiny realm of poetry and romance, all these combined to give such life and beauty to Scott's stanzas that I could say of this fair lake what a poet had written of the lady of his love:

> "As a perfume doth remain
> In the folds where it hath lain,
> So the thought of you remaining
> Deeply folded in my brain,
> Will not leave me; all else leaves me,
> You remain."

On leaving Loch Katrine and riding on among the wild and picturesque mountains that environ it, Sir Walter's memory still follows us at every step. One of the bristling peaks, for example, recalls the scene where the brave Knight Fitz James informed the stranger he had met, that he had sworn to some day face the rebel chieftain, Roderick Dhu, and all his miscreant band. Standing before the hillock, still called "Roderick's Watch-tower," we recollect that chieftain's answer:

LEAVING LOCH KATRINE.

> "'Have, then, thy wish!' He whistled shrill,
> And he was answer'd from the hill;
> Wild as the scream of the curlew,
> From crag to crag the signal flew.
> . . . .

TROSSACHS CHURCH, LOCH ACHRAY.

On right, on left, above, below,
Sprung up at once the lurking foe;
. . . .
And every tuft of broom gives life
To plaidèd warrior arm'd for strife.
That whistle garrison'd the glen
At once with full five hundred men.
The Mountaineer cast glance of pride
Along Ben Ledi's bristling side,
Then fix'd his eye and sable brow
Full on Fitz James: 'How say'st thou now?
These are Clan-Alpine's warriors true;
And, Saxon, I am Roderick Dhu!'"

Sometimes, however, in traveling among these lakes and mountain streams, we are diverted from the past to the present, and from poetry to a very practical pursuit. Hunting has largely disappeared from the Scottish Highlands, yet fishermen still have a chance to exercise their skill. But at what a cost! Can there be any pleasure in wading into the water, and soaking there for hours, merely to catch a cold,—sometimes a fish? I must confess that when I hear enthusiastic followers of Izaak Walton declare that such an experience is delightful, I feel inclined to reply, as a polite

NEAR RODERICK'S WATCHTOWER.

A SALMON POOL IN THE TROSSACHS.

Frenchman did, on hearing an incredible story, "No doubt you aire right, but God knows it ees imposseeble!"

The traveler, accustomed to the Alps, is apt to say, as he surveys the Trossachs, "There is no grandeur in the scenery of Scotland." Yet his opinion will inevitably change, when he beholds the mountains of Glencoe. The secret of their undeniable sublimity is not, however, their great height, since they rarely attain an elevation of four thousand feet above the sea. It is not even the impressive way in which they heave their monstrous masses westward, like gigantic waves. The grand effect which they produce is principally due to the forever changing clouds, which magnify their altitude by heaping up around and upon them, noiselessly and swiftly, enormous shapes which are themselves almost as large as the huge peaks they half conceal. Scotch mists are usually cold and unattractive; but, grouped in billowy immensity, around the mountains of

Glencoe they are sublime; and, when illumined by the glow of sunset, these northern vapors become radiantly beautiful; for the departing sun transforms them into fields of splendor, gilds all their gloomy heights with glory, and places upon Scotland's brow a crown of gold.

Edinburgh in the early part of this century was called the "Athens of the North." It was, indeed, the brain of Scotland, and on this northern firmament had suddenly appeared a galaxy of literary stars: Sir Walter Scott, Burns, Jeffrey, Hume, and Chambers, who gave the city an immortal fame. Still another reason for that title was furnished by the topographical resemblance between the capitals of Greece and Scotland. Both overlook the sea, and both have neighboring mountains which bear a striking similarity to one another in the relative positions they hold toward their respective cities. This is particularly noticeable in Edinburgh's Castle Rock, which rises from

THE MOUNTAINS OF GLENCOE.

the town as boldly and abruptly as the Acropolis from the city of Pericles. It is a pleasing, and certainly not an unprofitable, occupation for the tourist to sit at his hotel window, on Princes Street, and watch the lingering twilight of the North climb slowly up that perpendicular rock, and, finally, leave it in the care of Night, as it has done, day after day, so many million times since a caprice of Nature placed it there. As for the period of its history since man has had to do with it, it is of course the oldest portion of the city, — the starting-point of its development, and it was no doubt a fortress even before the conquest of the country by the Romans. It is another proof of what we find all over Europe, among the Alps and Apennines, through the Black Forest and along the Rhine, that every isolated crag or mountain peak was always utilized as a stronghold of defense, in the days when every man's hand seemed to be raised against his neighbor, and when life was based upon

PRINCES STREET, EDINBURGH.

EDINBURGH.

EDINBURGH CASTLE AND SCOTCH GUARDS.

"the plan
That he shall take who has the power,
And he shall keep who can."

What memories are hidden in the massive battlements of this abode of Scottish kings, like jewels in an iron casket! Along the steep path leading to the Castle gate, fair Mary, Queen of Scots, and many other royal visitors often passed. In one of its apartments poor Mary's only child was born, and from a window in these walls the little one was lowered several hundred feet in a basket, and thence conveyed in furious haste to Stirling Castle. What a strange introduction into the world, for one who finally became the King, not only of Scotland, but of England also, and thus at last consolidated the rival crowns!

In an apartment called the "Crown Room," and guarded by a metal cage reaching from floor to ceiling are the old, discarded souvenirs of Scottish sovereignty, including the crown

THE OLD TOWN, EDINBURGH.

once worn by Robert Bruce, the sword of State, the sceptre, and some splendid jewels. There was something profoundly sad to me in the sight of these abandoned relics of Scottish royalty. If this was to be the ending of all the centuries of warfare between the Scotch and English, of what avail was the loss of thousands of lives along the Border, the valiant deeds of Wallace, the heroism of Bruce, and the victories of Bannockburn and Flodden Field? But Time works marvels; and what would have been treason, or cowardice, in one century, may become good State policy in the next. Community of interests and mutual protection are often more potent than national prejudices, and sometimes bring about a change in public sentiment amounting almost to a revolution. Such prejudices, when removed by the broader, gentler spirit of humanity, resemble mighty icebergs which have been drifting southward from the Arctic Circle, threatening commerce with annihilation, and seeming to be indestructible from their enormous size and mountainous solidity; but which, yielding little by little to the warmer waters of the Gulf Stream, and the milder breezes from the tropics, finally, without a struggle, dissolve and disappear forever in the boundless sea.

A few years previous to Mary's execution, the idea of a union between Scotland and England would have been scouted by her former subjects, to whom the English seemed their bitterest foes. In fact, the claim of Mary to the throne of England brought her to the block; yet, strange to say, her child was welcomed as Elizabeth's successor.

The monument which Edinburgh has erected to Sir Walter Scott is probably the noblest tribute to purely literary genius that the world possesses. It is an exquisitely graceful Gothic spire of red sandstone more than two hundred feet in height. Its arches, turrets, and retreating pinnacles rise with consummate elegance and lightness toward the sky, and in its principal niches are figures representing characters in Scott's writings; while, in the centre, under this elaborate canopy, is a marble statue of Sir Walter himself, attended by his favorite dog. It is appropriate that, both in sculpture and painting, Scott should have been usually represented with a dog for his companion; for never was a man fonder of dogs than was the author of "Ivanhoe." When he was sojourning as an invalid in Naples, he wrote repeatedly to his steward at Abbotsford to be "very careful of

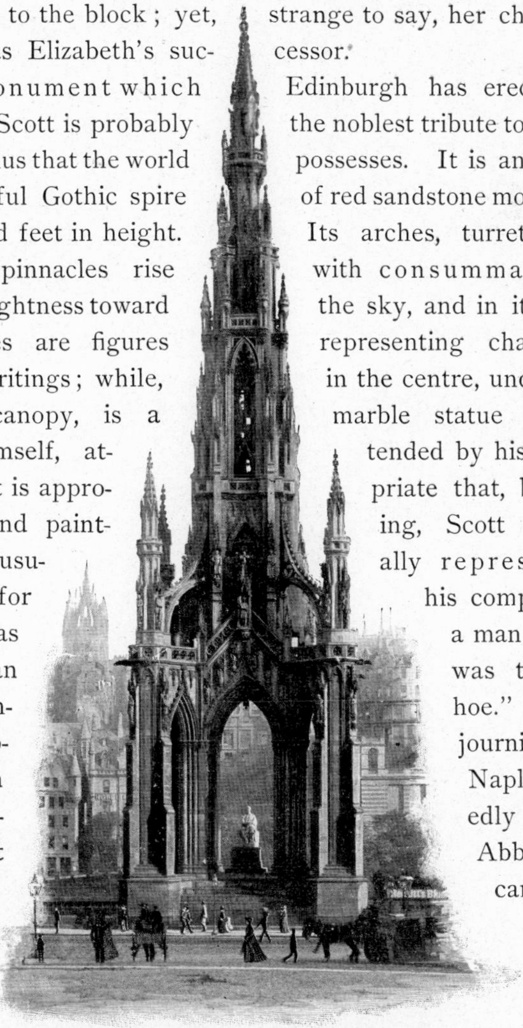

SCOTT'S MONUMENT, EDINBURGH.

the poor people, and the dogs." On his return, also, his meeting with his old favorites was quite touching; and when the last sad days arrived, as his dogs came around his chair and mutely licked his hands, their dying master said farewell to them with mingled smiles and tears. It is pleasing to remember, as one looks upon it, that subscriptions for this memorial to Scott's genius came from all classes of society, and if upon the list appears the contribution of one hundred pounds from Her Majesty, the Queen, one can read there, also, the donation of three pounds seven shillings "from the poor people of the Cowgate."

SIR WALTER'S STATUE.

Some years before Scott's death, on a hot summer day, the future architect of this magnificent structure, Mr. John M. Kemp, then a poor apprentice, was trudging along a dusty road carrying a heavy basket of tools. A carriage passed him going in the same direction. Within it was an elderly gentleman who, noticing his weary face, offered the lad a seat. The poor boy gratefully accepted; and while thus taking his first drive in a gentleman's carriage, the subsequent designer of this monument met for the only time in his life the celebrated author, with whose illustrious name his own was destined to acquire a lasting fame.

A journey of a few hours from Edinburgh brought us to the ruined edifice of which Sir Walter was so fond, — Melrose

Abbey. The first impression made upon me as I walked through its deserted corridors was that of overwhelming sadness at the vandalism which had destroyed it; for it is true of this, as of so many others of the world's great monuments, that man, not Nature, caused the ruin. Although constructed more than seven hundred years ago, it might be standing now in its entirety, had not the ravages of war, and of a still more pitiless religious fury, dealt here their cruel and destructive blows. No less than four English armies of invasion vented their fury on its walls; Cromwell actually bombarded it; and, finally, the followers of John Knox, in their mistaken zeal, defaced it with malicious joy. How much of its former beauty is, therefore, lost to us! The spacious windows, for example, were once encased in beautifully sculptured frames, whose exquisite stone carving seemed a reproduction, in elaborate garlands, of Nature's lovely handiwork in the adjoining fields.

A SCOTCH PIPER.

MELROSE ABBEY.

Now the windows are as bare and desolate as eyeless sockets, and only a few poor traces of their

THE GREAT WINDOW.

ornamentation still exist, where through exhaustion or caprice the vandals stayed their wearied hands; while the stained-glass figures of saints and prophets, which formerly peopled all these elegantly bordered spaces, in robes of ruby, orange, violet, green, and gold, have, like the thousands who once knelt beneath them, disappeared forever. Originally, too, this abbey had a roof of stone, as exquisitely carved as were the columns which upheld it; but that has, also, long since vanished, and now its only covering is the dome of heaven. Through these abandoned aisles the winds of many centuries have

A CORNER OF THE ABBEY.

blown; where flags of brave crusaders proudly waved, masses of weeds and ivy flutter in the breeze; the only footsteps here, to-day, are those of travelers; the only incense on its ruined altar is the breath of the wild rose.

GRAVE OF THE WIZARD, MICHAEL SCOTT.

One object, however, has escaped destruction. It is a beautifully sculptured window, carved in the likeness of the crown of thorns which Roman soldiers placed derisively upon the head of Christ. It is an admirable work of art. Even in stone, the cruel points turn down as if to sink profoundly into the bleeding flesh. The pious hands which wrought this masterpiece have crumbled into dust. The eyes which gazed upon it, doubtless, often dimmed with

THE CROWN OF THORNS WINDOW.

SIR WALTER SCOTT.

tears, have long ago been closed in death; yet where all else has perished, this survives. Before this symbol of majestic suffering, even the hands of desecrators faltered powerless. Itself the crown of this imposing ruin, its thorns are still, as they have been for centuries, the souvenir of a divine self-sacrifice, its perfect circle the emblem of eternity. The interest of Melrose Abbey is not confined, however, to its architecture; for in one part of the building lies buried the heart of the valiant Robert Bruce, and it also contains the grave of the warlike Douglas, and that of the reputed wizard, Michael Scott. Every reader of the "Lay of the Last Minstrel" will remember that this is the spot alluded to by Sir Walter when he describes the visit to Melrose Abbey of William of Deloraine, who had come to wrest from the dead necromancer's withered hand his book of

MELROSE ABBEY, FROM THE CHURCHYARD.

ABBOTSFORD, FROM THE RIVER.

magic; and it was through these windows, once so glorious with color, that

> "The silver light so pale and faint
> Showed many a prophet and many a saint,"

as the awe-stricken chieftain watched till a moonbeam fell directly on the wizard's grave, and thus gave warning that the fearful hour had come when he could safely take from the dead man's grasp the secret of his power.

Leaving this charming ruin, a drive of three miles through a pretty, undulating country brought us to Abbotsford, the home of Scott. It is delightfully situated on a terrace, just above the Tweed; in fact, so near it, that the murmur of the river in its rocky bed can be distinctly heard through the open windows. This tract of country possessed for Scott a peculiar fascination. It had belonged in former times to the old Abbots of Melrose, and near it were the ruins of the Abbey which he

ABBOTSFORD, SOUTH FRONT.

loved so well. When he first bought the property, he lived upon it in a modest cottage; but, as his wealth increased, he built a veritable castle of red sandstone trimmed with granite, where he, subsequently, resided and which became his joy and pride. It was his own creation, and every part of it was intended to recall to him some tower or romantic ruin which he had admired and described. He likened it, therefore, to one of his romances carved in stone. Not long, however, was he destined to remain here in undisturbed enjoyment. The very year in which it was completed beheld the terrible financial crisis which, with the sudden fury of a cyclone, wrecked his fortune and in a single day transformed him into a pauper.

One winter's morning, in 1826, a friend arrived at Abbotsford and found the novelist in great mental agitation. As he approached, Sir Walter said to him: "My friend, give me your hand, mine is that of a beggar"; for, in truth, the publishing house with which the author had been long connected had,

THE HALL.

through no fault of his, failed with enormous liabilities. From that time on, Scott's life became heroic and his character sublime. If he had chosen to act as many insolvent merchants do, the matter could have been quickly settled, but Scott regarded his pecuniary troubles from the standpoint of honor. He thought that by devoting the rest of his life to his creditors, he could, finally, pay them every farthing that he owed, and he succeeded. But at what a cost! There are few sadder things on earth than the poverty of old age; few more pathetic sights than that of an old man who has lost the fortune, acquired laboriously through his earlier years, to shelter him in the decline of life and to provide for those most dear to him. For, when

THE DRAWING-ROOM.

SCOTT'S STUDY.

the shadows of life's fleeting day are falling eastward, and the hush of evening steals upon the world, it ought to be an old man's privilege to rest; and it is pitiful to see him, then, wearily groping in the twilight for treasures which he should have harvested and garnered in the heat of day. This, however, was exactly what Scott was obliged to do. At the time of the failure he was fifty-five years old, and his obligations amounted to six hundred thousand dollars; yet this enormous sum he earned and paid off in six years, by the unceasing labor of his brain. But, alas! he gave his life to save his honor. Twelve, fourteen, sixteen hours a day he toiled through those six years of failing strength and premature old age. What had once been a joyous

SCOTT'S LIBRARY.

SCOTT'S "OWN ROMANTIC TOWN."

occupation, became at last a struggle similar to that of General Grant, when he kept Death at bay till he had finished dictating his memoirs. At last, in 1832, shortly before his death, he wrote: "I think I shall never walk again; but I must not complain, for my plan of settling my debts has been, thank God, completely successful, and I have paid one hundred and twenty thousand pounds, without owing any one a ha'penny."

Nothing in Scott's career is more touching than his last attempt to work. Though very ill, he begged his daughters to bring him ink and paper, and to put the pen into his trembling hand. They did so, and he smiled and thanked them; but when he tried to write, his fingers could not hold the pen. It dropped upon the page. The old hero sank back in his chair. He did not speak and tears rolled down his cheeks. At length he murmured, "Don't let me expose my weakness here. Get me — get me to bed. That's the only place now."

BUST OF SCOTT.

In the long library at Abbotsford Sir Walter's marble bust looks out upon the visitor from the dark background of his favorite books. It is a kindly, noble face. No wonder Scotland venerates the memory of this man. Humanity admires him as well. Here certainly was one whom Nature framed to bear "the grand old name of gentleman." To me, as I beheld the symmetry and beauty of this work of art, it seemed a symbol of the fact that as the sculptor's strokes had caused it to emerge from a rough block of marble, so by adversity's relentless blows the poet's soul had been developed, from an untried and formless character, into one made perfect through suffering.

ROOM WHERE SIR WALTER DIED.

It was in the dining-room at Abbotsford that Sir Walter died. He had requested that his bed be made up here, because from this room he could most plainly hear the murmur of the river. "It was a beautiful day," writes his biographer, "so warm, that every window was wide open, and so perfectly still, that the sound of all others most delicious to his ear, the gentle ripple of the Tweed over its pebbles, was distinctly audible." Here, then, at the age of sixty-one, and attended by all his children, his gentle spirit passed away from earth; and while his family knelt around his bed, his eldest son kissed and closed his eyes. "No

AN ARCH IN DRYBURGH ABBEY.

sculptor," says Lockhart, "ever modeled a more majestic image of repose."

A wonderful procession was that which followed Scott's body to the grave. Mourners had come from every part of Scotland. The line of carriages alone was more than a mile in length. Hundreds of yeomanry followed on horseback. In every village on the way the entire population stood before their doorways, clothed in black. The heavens, too, were hung with clouds, as if in lamentation for the poet's death. Those who observed this, must have remembered Scott's own language, in the touching lines:

> "Call it not vain; they do not err
> Who say that when the Poet dies,
> Mute Nature mourns her worshiper
> And celebrates his obsequies;
> Who say tall cliff and cavern lone
> For the departed Bard make moan;
> That mountains weep in crystal rill;
> That flowers in tears of balm distill:
> . . . .
> And rivers teach their rushing wave
> To murmur dirges round his grave."

DRYBURGH ABBEY.

SCOTT'S TOMB.

The tower beneath which Scotland's greatest genius lies in dreamless sleep forms a part of Dryburgh Abbey, a beautiful old ruin, the history of which extends back more than seven hundred years. Here, also, are the graves of his beloved wife, his son, and his son-in-law Lockhart, who wrote the story of his life. It is a touching proof of the love which Scott inspired in all around him, that those who brought his body to this, its final resting-place, were his old, faithful servants, who, with tears in their eyes, had begged that only they might be allowed to pay the master they so dearly loved this last sad service.

IVY-MANTLED WINDOW, DRYBURGH.

Within this

ON THE DEE.

ruined abbey, hallowed by Sir Walter's dust, is an ivy-mantled window which he especially admired. Standing before it, as he had often done, and thinking of the noble life which I had followed to its end, I called to mind, as a beautiful illustration of his character, the memorable words uttered by him shortly before his death: "I am drawing near to the close of my career. I am fast shuffling off the stage. I have been, perhaps, the most voluminous author of the day; and it is a comfort to me to think that I have tried to unsettle no man's faith, to corrupt no man's principles, and that I have written nothing which, on my death-bed, I should wish blotted."

I have often thought, that if I might liken the history of Scotland to its natural scenery: its wild ravines and rugged mountains would be symbols of the daring deeds of Bruce and Wallace; its countless lakes and rivulets would call to mind the infinitely varied, sparkling lines of Robert Burns; its lovely landscapes would suggest the elaborate descriptions of Sir Walter Scott; and all the flowers on the Scottish hills, which lift into the light and

DRYBURGH ABBEY, FROM THE WEST.

air their perfume and their beauty, would serve as emblems of fair Mary, Queen of Scots.

MARY.

One summer, having in previous years explored Europe thoroughly along the beaten tracks, I resolved to take up, as a special biographical subject, the life of Mary Stuart, and to follow her footsteps from her cradle at Linlithgow to the place of her execution at Fotheringay, in order thus to realize more vividly, and as far as possible chronologically, the thrilling episodes of her career. Leaving Edinburgh, therefore, at the outset, I went directly to Linlithgow Castle. On the 7th of December, 1542, this palace echoed to rejoicings over the advent of a little princess. It is true, the joy would have been greater had the child been a boy, and the King, her father, who was on his death-bed, on learning of her sex, exclaimed: "Woe to the crown of Scotland: it came with a girl and it will go with a girl"; but, notwithstanding their disappointment, the child was dear to all true Scottish hearts, for she was the sole survivor of the royal line, the infant heiress of the realm.

IN QUEEN MARY'S COUNTRY.

Although Linlithgow Castle is at present nothing but a picturesque old ruin, one may yet stand within the very room (now desolate and roofless) which saw the advent of the infant princess. The walls of the building were, evidently, of great strength and thickness; but they were not deemed strong enough at that time to protect the future

LINLITHGOW CASTLE.

queen. War was then being waged between Scotland and England, and Henry VIII. was using every means to get this little princess into his blood-stained hands; for by his third unfortunate wife, whom he had wedded only a few hours after the ax had fallen on the neck of Anne Boleyn, he now possessed a son. This prince, he had resolved, should marry Mary, Queen of Scots, and thus unite the kingdoms under one crown. The terms of his proposal, however, were so harsh that Scotland's Parliament refused them, and in the conflict which ensued, both Mary and her mother were taken for greater security from Linlithgow to Stirling Castle. Surely no safer nor more healthful place could have been found for her than this grand fortress, towering on a lofty cliff above the enchanting valley of Monteith. Yet, even here, though the child thrived in the pure mountain air, dangers and intrigues threatened her on every side, since the English King regarded her with hatred because both she and Scotland's liberty had not been given to him submissively.

THE QUADRANGLE, LINLITHGOW CASTLE.

A plot was formed whereby some of her own treacherous nobles were to visit Stirling, profess a great desire to see the child, and then if Mary was produced, to seize and carry her off to England; but so extremely cautious were her guardians, that only one visitor was ever admitted at a time to see her, and even then in the presence of armed men. We cannot, therefore, be surprised that, with all these dangers threatening her, the coronation of the little Queen was solemnized as soon as possible. One Sunday morning, when she was nine months old, Mary was taken from her nursery, and with much solemn pageantry was carried into the chapel of the castle. There one of her nobles held her on the throne,

STIRLING CASTLE.

STATUE OF WALLACE, STIRLING CASTLE.

and spoke for her the words which her young lips could not yet frame. Then the Cardinal held the crown over her infant brow, clasped for a moment her tiny fingers about the sceptre, and even buckled round her waist the sword of State. How strange the contrast between the pretty, helpless babe, and all the mailèd men surrounding her, bearing the implements of royalty and war! Alas! though every peer and prelate present knelt before the child, held his right hand above her little head, and swore to defend her with his life, how few of them kept the oath!

HOLYROOD CASTLE.

A volume would hardly suffice to trace in sequence and detail the strange events of Mary's life; but every traveler who feels the slightest interest in her his-

LORD DARNLEY'S ROOM, HOLYROOD CASTLE.

tory visits, at least, her principal place of residence, Holyrood Castle, at Edinburgh. Within the chapel of this building, at the age of twenty-three, Mary was married to Lord Darnley. There is no doubt that she loved him; for when, on the death in France of her youthful husband, Francis II., she returned to Scotland, she had no lack of suitors. They fairly flocked to her, and every royal bachelor and widower in Christendom was not without some hope of winning her for a wife. She gave her heart and hand, however, to Lord Darnley, whom she declared to be "the handsomest long man" she had ever seen.

HOLYROOD CASTLE AND CHAPEL.

It was a hasty, reckless marriage, like many others made before and since that time; for men and women do not seem to grow much wiser in this respect. A few weeks were enough to render all too plain her husband's character. Up to the time of the wedding Darnley had managed to conceal his faults; but having secured his prize, he boldly showed the vanity and selfishness which in reality controlled his conduct. Mary (besides the precious privilege of her love) had given him every honor in her power to grant; yet Darnley, with detestable ingratitude, took all these favors as a matter of course, and coolly asked for more, — demanding nothing less than equal sovereignty with her. The English ambassador wrote of them soon after their marriage: "The Queen doth everything in her power to oblige Darnley; but Darnley does not do the least thing to oblige her." It is pathetic to reflect that Mary's whole career might have been changed, if she had wedded a different kind of man; for the heart of a woman like Mary resembles a blank page on which one hand, and only one, may write Fate's stern decree of happiness or woe. She was a

IN THE INTERIOR OF SCOTLAND.

woman whom the right marital influence would have encouraged to the noblest deeds; and she was, doubtless, well aware of this and, seeing her irreparable error, became sad and reckless. She had, however, a few weeks of happiness during her wedding journey through the interior of Scotland; and in the long years of her subsequent captivity how often must she have recalled those hours of bliss, and wondered (as many beside her have done) why, at some supreme crisis in life, when the soul has drunk its fill of the golden wine of perfect happiness, we cannot slip away from earth, beyond the possibility of change, before the color fades and the perfume vanishes, and, thrilled with the remembrance of that last precious moment, enter, at least, the paradise of memory, which is the only paradise that is never lost. But it was Mary's fate to linger on for years, realizing more and more keenly with each bitter disillusion what her life might have been under other conditions. Oh, the lost days and years of wasted opportunities! Alas, for the rich treasures left buried beyond finding by the stream that has passed! The evil character of Mary's husband was not merely negative. It soon displayed itself in the brutal treatment of his wife. Only four months after their wedding,

COURTYARD, HOLYROOD CASTLE.

LOCH LOMOND.

at a public banquet, Darnley began to drink to excess, and urged the other guests to follow his example. When Mary endeavored quietly to check him, he turned upon her with such vulgar violence that she withdrew from the company in tears.

So insolent, also, was his conduct toward the Court in general that he was almost universally detested. Among the many enemies whom Darnley made, by his harsh treatment of the Queen, was Rizzio. It was in the chapel of Holyrood Castle that Mary's attention was first drawn to Rizzio. One winter's day, a mass was being celebrated there, and, suddenly, in the midst of the service, Mary heard, ringing through the aisles, a rich, sonorous voice of wonderful power and sweetness. She inquired who the new singer was. They told her that he was an Italian, the private secretary of the ambassador from Savoy, and that his name was Rizzio. The Queen, whose taste in music was of the finest, requested that he should henceforth lead the singing in her chapel services. Every one knows the famous painting by David Neal, portraying the meeting of the Queen and Rizzio. The artist represents him as a handsome, finely-formed Italian, carelessly sleeping at her palace gate; but was he really thus attractive? Historians of the time describe him as a man without the slightest claim to beauty. Is this the truth, or did those writers so represent

MEETING OF MARY AND RIZZIO.

BOTHWELL CASTLE.

him in order that the story of Mary's love for him should seem improbable? Well, that is a part of the enigma, which now at every step grows more mysterious. One thing at least is certain, Rizzio's musical skill and splendid voice made him a most agreeable member of the Court. Nor were these his only talents. He had the diplomatic tact so characteristic of his nation, he was a clever linguist, and his fidelity and prudence were undoubted. Perceiving all these qualities, Mary made Rizzio her private secretary.

To understand the history of the hapless Queen of Scots, it should be remembered that almost all the nobles who surrounded her were treacherous, unprincipled men who shrank from the commission of no crime that would enable them to govern Scotland as they liked, by making the actual sovereign a cipher in their hands. Among these Scottish lords there was now formed one of the most atrocious schemes which even the villainy of the Middle Ages ever framed. They had long wanted to be rid of Rizzio, because he was not one of them yet had such influence with the Queen; but what excuse could justify his murder? Plainly enough, — an injured husband's honor. Darnley was to profess himself jealous of the favorite, and, as an evidence of his guilt, Rizzio was to be slain in Mary's presence.

Was there really cause for Darnley to be suspicious of Rizzio, as Mary's lover? On the contrary, there are strong reasons to prove such a theory highly improbable. First, no charge of the kind existed when Darnley married Mary, which seems to dispose of the time before her wedding. Secondly, Mary undoubtedly married Darnley from love, and it was less than a year after the wedding that Rizzio was murdered. Thirdly, the shrewd Italian had worked in every way to bring about the union of the Queen and Darnley, believing it to be for Mary's interest; and it was actually in Rizzio's private room at Stirling Castle that, in order to outwit their enemies, their secret marriage had taken place, some months before the public wedding in Holyrood Chapel. Far from disliking him, therefore, Darnley was at first very grateful to the young Italian, and looked upon him as his friend. But now affairs were changed; for, in the disputes which had arisen about increasing Darnley's power in State affairs, Rizzio, faithful to the Queen, invariably took her part. Darnley, therefore, believing him to be the greatest obstacle to his ambitious projects, longed for his destruction. It is evident, then, that political motives are sufficient to explain the whole affair; for Rizzio's death was but the opening step of a profound conspiracy into which Darnley had been coaxed and flattered. He was still a boy, hardly out of his

A RUINED STRONGHOLD.

teens, and a mere puppet in the hands of the crafty men who took advantage of his folly to further their ambitious schemes. It was possible that this abominable plot to murder Rizzio in Mary's presence might endanger her own life and that of her unborn child; but what mattered it? If she should die, so much the better for them! If she survived the shock, she was to be imprisoned, — possibly, forced to abdicate; while Darnley, although nominally king, would still remain an insignificant figurehead, behind which the conspirators would really rule.

HAPPINESS DWELLETH NOT IN PALACES.

Into the courtyard of Holyrood Castle, just after dusk, on the night appointed for the crime, Mary's Lord Chancellor, Morton (one of the chief conspirators), led a body of armed men. A number of these desperados hid themselves in Darnley's room, above which were the Queen's apartments, whither a winding staircase led. It was seven o'clock. Mary was in her library at supper. Three friends, a lady, a gentleman, and Rizzio, were her guests. Suddenly Darnley, who had come up the private stairway, entered the supper-room. Seating himself in a vacant chair beside his wife, he put his arm around her waist, and gave her an affectionate kiss. It was the kiss of Judas; for, meantime, his associates following him had stolen softly into Mary's bedroom. Impatient of delay, they crowded through the doorway into the Queen's presence. Mary, alarmed, demanded what their intrusion signified. They said they meant no harm to her, but only to the villain near her. Rizzio saw that his hour had come. "Madam," he said to his sovereign, "I am lost." "Fear not," she answered firmly, "the King will never suffer you to be slain in my presence, nor can he forget your many faithful services." At this appeal, which probably touched a tender spot in Darnley's heart, he faltered, apparently unwilling to perform his part. "Sir," exclaimed Ruthven fiercely,

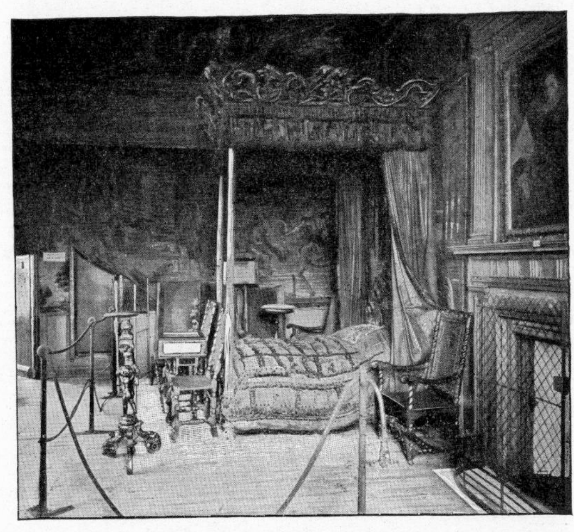

MARY'S BEDROOM.

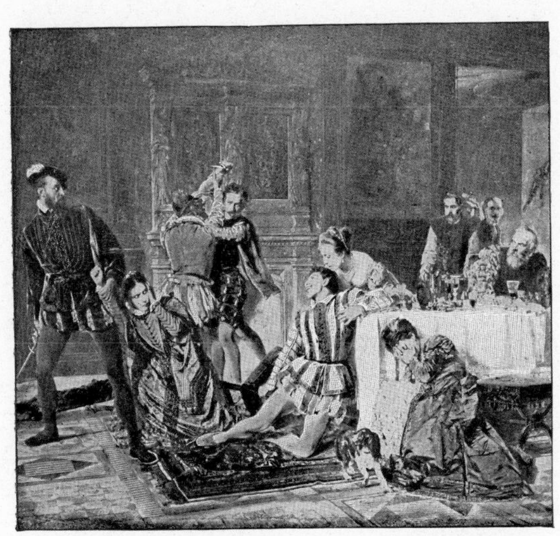

MURDER OF RIZZIO.

THE SPOT WHERE RIZZIO WAS SLAIN.

"look to your wife and sovereign." At this Darnley forced Mary into a chair and held her there so tightly that she could not rise. One of the ruffians presented a pistol to her side, and with a horrible oath swore he would shoot her dead if she resisted. "Fire," she dauntlessly replied, "if you have no respect for my own life, or for that of my unborn child." Her husband pushed away the weapon. Meantime the supper-room was lighted with the glare of torches, and echoed to the tread of other murderous invaders. Rizzio, clinging to the Queen's dress, piteously cried: "Save my life, Madam! Save my life, for God's dear sake!" The assassins rushed upon him. A terrible scene ensued. The table with its lights and dishes was overturned. Mary fainted. At last the frantic clutch of Rizzio on Mary's robe relaxed, and he was dragged out into a narrow passageway and stabbed repeatedly, until his shrieks were hushed in death. Those who have visited Holyrood will recollect the stain upon the floor said to have been caused by his blood.

As for Mary, when all the uproar had subsided, and she had partially regained her senses, her lawless nobles told her that she was their prisoner, and, setting a guard at her door, they left her to spend the night in horror, anxiety, and fear. Is it any wonder if, after such an experience as this, Mary's character was somewhat changed? There are some natures which resemble water, — tractable enough when they flow in their appointed channels; but, when congealed by coldness, they freeze and cannot be bent. They may indeed be broken, but that ruins them.

Upon a little island in one of the most beautiful of Scottish lakes — Lochleven — stands the prison of Queen Mary. For, at last, her enemies dethroned her. Two of her nobles, in the dead of night, took her from Edinburgh Castle, placed her upon a horse, and made her ride with them for several hours at full gallop, until at dawn she found herself upon the borders of this lake. Without delay she was conveyed across the water to the castle, where two of the murderers of Rizzio (well calculated, therefore, to inspire her with fear) threatened to drown her in the lake if she did not immediately sign her abdication in favor of her son, and name one of their

LOCHLEVEN.

number, the Earl of Murray, Regent, till the boy became of age. This, in her desperate condition, Mary was obliged to do. Having played, therefore, their last and most successful card, the game was won and Mary's foes withdrew in triumph, leaving her here a broken-hearted captive.

The thrilling episode of her escape from Lochleven is as exciting as a romance. Some months had passed since Mary

LOCHLEVEN CASTLE.

had been forced to abdicate. Day after day had dragged monotonously on, like shadows on the castle walls. At last, however, there came a change. One Sunday night the Queen stood at her window watching the lake intently. Her eager scrutiny was at length rewarded. She saw a small boat approaching the island noiselessly. Within it was a young man named George Douglas. He was the son of her jailer; but both he and his younger brother, enamoured of the lovely captive, had sworn to risk their lives in her behalf. It is

SWAN ISLAND, LOCH LOMOND.

another proof that the explanation of half the history of the world is love. While this was going on, the other members of the Douglas family were at supper. Among them was William, the accomplice of his brother George. The castle keys were lying on the table. William contrived to drop a napkin over them, lifted them noiselessly, and left the room. Five minutes later the family had been locked in, as captives; Mary's door had been opened; the keys had been thrown into the lake; the two young men were rowing to the land with all their might; and with them sat the fairest woman in all Scotland, — Mary, Queen of Scots, leaving this hated prison forever.

LOCHLEVEN BY MOONLIGHT.

Poor, beautiful, Queen Mary! the fascinating story of her tragic life imparts an interest and pathos to everything connected with her memory. Thus, of the crumbling castle of Lochleven, a poet has well sung:

> "No warden's fire shall e'er again
> Illume Lochleven's bosom fair;
> No clarion shrill of armèd men
> The breeze across the lake shall bear;
> But while remains a stone of thine,
> It shall be linked to royal fame, —
> For here the Rose of Stuart's line
> Hath left the fragrance of her name."

Not long, however, did the Queen enjoy her freedom. A few weeks later her faithful followers were defeated by the army of the Regent, and Mary was again a fugitive. For two days she remained in old Dundrennan Abbey, in anxious consultation with her few attendants. What should be done? Mary herself desired to go to England and appeal to Elizabeth for help. Her friends, however, fearing that Queen's duplicity and jealousy, advised her to escape to France. This, doubtless, would have proved the wiser plan; but Mary trusted to the friendly words which had been sent by Elizabeth during her captivity at Lochleven. Accordingly she crossed the English frontier and rashly confided herself to the royal cousin who had, from first to last, invariably been her foe.

DUNDRENNAN ABBEY.

It is hard to realize that Mary's captivity in England lasted almost three times as long as her whole Scottish reign; but it is true that, having been Queen of Scotland only seven years, she was Elizabeth's prisoner nineteen. Yet what a mistake, as well as crime, was this unjust imprisonment! Her lovely form seen through her prison bars made her at once a heroine and martyr, and touched ten thousand hearts with sympathy. Her old claim to the English throne, thus constantly suggested, gave rise to scores of plots whereby the Catholic party tried to regain supremacy. Of many of them Mary undoubtedly knew nothing; but since her name was always used, and her release was an essential feature of each scheme, the Protestant reformers hated her relentlessly, and urged Elizabeth to take her life. At last, a new conspiracy was discovered, in which the unhappy prisoner seemed implicated, so far at least as trying to regain her liberty. She was, however, accused of treason and of a wish to assassinate Elizabeth. Mary protested against the right of any English court to judge her (since she was not a subject of Elizabeth, but an independent sovereign), but the English earls and barons who composed her judges pronounced her guilty, and Parliament sentenced her to death. It only remained for Elizabeth to decide whether or not the sentence should be carried into effect.

ELIZABETH.

What must have been the captive's suffering during those last months of suspense, when the decree of Parliament was known, and while Elizabeth still hesitated to enforce it! It is comparatively easy to prepare for execution once. It is a different thing to have the sword continually suspended over one's head. Mary, however, made no appeal for mercy. Whatever was to be her fate, she was resolved to meet it like a Queen. Few epi-

THE FAIR PRISONER.

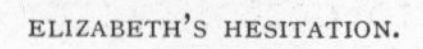

ELIZABETH'S HESITATION.

sodes in history are more pathetic than the final scene in Fotheringay Castle. As Mary approached the block, every one was impressed by the melancholy sweetness of her face, and by the traces of that rare personal beauty which had contributed so much to the sorrows of her life. Even her executioners knelt down and asked forgiveness for the duty which they must perform. The Queen replied, "I forgive you and all the world with all my heart." Then turning to the women who attended her, she exclaimed: "Pray do not weep. Believe me, I am happy to leave the world. Tell my son" (here for an instant her voice faltered) "that I thought of him in my last moments, and that I sincerely hope his life may be happier than mine."

Finally, amid a dreadful silence, broken only by an occasional sob, Mary knelt down and laid her neck upon the block. A moment later her head was held up by the chief executioner with the words: "So perish all the enemies of Queen Elizabeth!"

LAST MOMENTS OF MARY.

Yes, Mary had perished; but there survived her the memorable words that she had uttered to her judges when on trial for her life: "I am a Queen, subject to none but God. Him do I call to witness that I am innocent of all the charges brought against me. And recollect, my lords, the theatre of the world is wider than the realm of England!" From the tribunal of Elizabeth Mary had thus appealed to the tribunal of humanity; and not in vain. Twenty years later, when her son was sovereign of both England and Scotland, he caused his mother's body to be removed from Fotheringay to London, and buried there with pomp and splendor. Shortly before this act of filial duty and respect, the death of England's queen had, also, in turn its element of tragedy. For, stricken with horror at the thought of her approaching dissolution, and struggling fiercely to retain vitality, Elizabeth had been unwilling till the very last to lie in bed, but had met the King of Terrors on the floor, as in an arena, where she fought for life.

MARY GOING TO THE BLOCK.

Elizabeth and Mary! The rival cousins now lie, almost side by side, beneath the same cathedral roof; and not a day goes by, or has gone by for centuries, but pilgrims to Westminster stand between their graves, questioning sadly the motives which inspired each, admiring the good which both achieved, and sighing in pity for the faults which both committed.

"No further seek [their] merits to disclose,
Nor draw [their] frailties from their dread abode;
There they alike in trembling hope repose,
The bosom of [their] Father and [their] God."

After such tragic memories of human suffering it is a pleasure to approach the western coast of Scotland, and study there with reverence and astonishment the works of God. The memories of Wallace, Bruce, Sir Walter, Burns, and Mary, Queen of Scots, are not the only fascinations which make a tour in Scotland so delightful. Apart from the human element, which interests us so deeply, this little country of the North has many points of natural scenery which may be justly called sublime.

MARY'S TOMB, WESTMINSTER ABBEY.

Nowhere in all my travels, not even among the fjords of Norway, have I seen a coast so strangely cleft and shattered into fragments, by the ocean surges, as the western shore of Scotland. For a long distance out to sea, the mountainous formation of the land continues; but through the valleys and ravines between those ocean-girdled hills the waves roll fathoms deep; and the great bluffs, swept naked by the blasts, rise from the seething flood, gaunt, bleak, and terrible, like the surviving monsters of some fearful deluge, turned to stone. At other

A HIGHLAND MILL.

THE EDGE OF THE ATLANTIC.

times, one sees along the bases of the wave-worn cliffs a multitude of sharply pointed rocks, like bones which the rapacious sea has left. Once they were, no doubt, portions of the habitable shore; but now they only serve as targets for the lightning's bolts or the sharp javelins of the western winds.

Especially conspicuous for desolate grandeur, off this western coast, are the Scotch islands called the Hebrides, the Ultima Thule of the ancient world. Two of them well repay a visit: Iona, for its history; and Staffa, for its scenery. The annals of Iona are unique and marvelous. It is only a barren rock, about two and a half miles long; yet there is hardly an island on the globe whose history is more remarkable.

More than thirteen hundred years ago, when on our English-speaking race the light of

"BONES LEFT BY THE RAPACIOUS SEA."

Christianity had scarcely dawned, and when Great Britain was still largely peopled by savages, there one day approached this island, from the coast of Ireland, a frail boat made of hides stretched over ribs of wood. This little skiff contained Columba, a Celtic missionary, and twelve disciples who, subsequently, founded here a monastery which was for centuries a monument of learning and religion, the spiritual light of the northwestern world, towering like a beacon fire above the sea of ignorance and barbarism, and causing Iona to be revered throughout all Europe as the "Holy Isle." Time and again the Scottish coast was ravaged by Norwegian pirates, who, usually, had no respect for either piety or learning; but such were the sanctity and fame of Iona, that it was the only place in Scotland spared by the northern chieftain Magnus III. in his career of plunder, and from the portal of Columba's church he is said to have recoiled with superstitious fear, not daring to enter the sacred edifice. The principal structure now remaining here was erected more than

THE TOURIST STEAMER, AT IONA.

IONA CATHEDRAL AND ROYAL GRAVEYARD.

eight hundred years ago, and marks the spot on which the earliest church was built.

But what impressed me even more than this was the ancient graveyard of Iona, whither for more than a thousand years, chieftains and kings of Scotland, Ireland, and even the far-off shores of Norway were conveyed for burial, partly on account of the reverence inspired by Columba's name, partly because it was believed that though, at the last day, every other island in the world might be engulfed, Iona would remain secure from all assaults of the invading sea. Among the forty kings of Scotland here entombed is the ill-fated Duncan, and close beside him rests his murderer, Macbeth, whose name has been immortalized by Shakespeare. One of the monuments in this ancient cemetery is a cross, cut from a single block of red granite, fourteen feet in height and covered with Runic inscriptions. It is the only perfect one remaining out of three hundred and sixty once erected here. Standing beside it, a feeling of awe stole over me, as I gazed upon Iona's line of royal sepulchres, and thought of the time when, century after century, numberless vessels crossed the northern seas to bring to this remote and isolated rock, not only the bodies of dead kings, but a multitude of pious pilgrims eager to pay homage to the Holy Isle; or warriors, branded with the curse of Cain, desiring absolution for their deeds of blood; or sovereigns seeking consecration at Columba's shrine. To-day, however, although the faith proclaimed here by Columba has been for centuries the religion of Europe, this island, which was once its most important northern starting-point, has sunk into obscurity and is almost uninhabited. Invaluable in its time, Christianity has nevertheless long since outgrown it; and poor Iona, therefore, rich alone in memories of the past, reminded me of Holmes' inspiring lines upon the "Chambered Nautilus":

RUNIC CROSS, IONA.

"Build thee more stately mansions, O my soul,
As the swift seasons roll!
Leave thy low-vaulted past!
Let each new temple, nobler than the last,
Shut thee from heaven with a dome more vast,
Till thou at length art free,
Leaving thine outgrown shell by life's unresting sea!"

A HIGHLAND HAMLET.

But, if Iona is interesting, Staffa is sublime. It is a child of Nature merely, wholly uninhabited by man, but its extraordinary natural phenomena bring travelers hither from all portions of the world. Twice have I seen it: once in storm, and once in sunshine. On both occasions it was wonderfully impressive; for, with a rounded form about two miles in circuit, it rises perpendicularly from the sea to the height of one hundred and forty

THE CLIFFS AT STAFFA.

feet; and its broad, level summit resembles an enormous table, upheld by thousands of basaltic columns, which stand in stately colonnades, pressed closely one against another, and in some places even curved slightly outward, as if to offer more resistance to the tremendous surges of the sea. This island, which is probably the crest of an extinct volcano, appeared to me the appropriate cradle of Scandinavian mythology. It is around just such a lonely, uninhabited rock, beaten for ages by the billows of the ocean, that the grand Sagas of the North would naturally cluster; for the old Norse myths are strong and heroic. They have a savage grandeur that is lacking in the legends of other races. While not possessing the subtile beauty of Greek and Roman mythology, they are, nevertheless, immeasurably more virile, dominant and fateful. There is only one "Twilight of the Gods," and it belongs to the land of Thor.

STAFFA.

The grandest feature of the island of Staffa, and, indeed, one of the most extraordinary objects in the world, is the awe-inspiring cavern, known as "Fingal's Cave," after the legendary Gaelic hero, Fingal. As our boat halted on its solemn threshold, the sound of voices ceased. The entire company seemed breathless. Before us, massive as the

BASALTIC COLUMNS, STAFFA.

eternal hills, rose a gigantic arch, sixty-five feet above the waves. Beneath this, leading on mysteriously toward the island's heart, lay a dark, undulating avenue whose terminus we could not see. To right and left, in serried ranks, stood hundreds of black, glistening columns of volcanic rock, worn smooth and lustrous by the waves which, for unnumbered ages, have been slowly eating out the softer stone of the interior, leaving the lofty arch and groinèd roof supported by basaltic pillars, tem-

THE APPROACH TO FINGAL'S CAVE.

pered in lava fire when the earth was young. Slowly we drew on toward the sombre portal, and as we halted in its awful shadow, and gazed on into the long gallery, the sides of which were black (save where the spectral fingers of the spray traced mystic characters upon the walls in lines of foam), I felt that nervous chill, that quick involuntary catching of the breath, which mark a recognition of sublimity. It seemed, indeed, a temple fashioned by Almighty God to give to man a model for his noblest shrines.

But oh! above all else that I remember here was the grand voice of the Atlantic in this cavern. After each wave, ere its successor could approach, there came an awful pause, in which the ocean seemed to hold its breath. Then, as the sea surged inward once more from the mighty deep, and swept its liquid touch along the stately colonnades, as if they were the strings of an Æolian harp, we heard the most unearthly and soul-stirring harmony: first, low and tender; then, swelling into a magnificent crescendo; and, finally, filling the whole cavern with an overpowering diapason that rolled like peals of thunder through the gloomy vault.

THE ENTRANCE.

At length, we passed on far into the cave, and, turning, looked back toward the sea. As, motionless and speechless, I surveyed it, the thought which thrilled me to the heart was this: that Nature, heedless of man's presence or existence, moves grandly on in her appointed path, obedient to Divine command; for, far away on this northwestern limit of the world, the waves had echoed thus when Egypt reared her pyramids, and Greece and Rome were yet unborn; the same sad requiem was chanted when Jesus hung upon the Cross; empires, dynasties, civilizations even, have risen, flourished, and decayed, while the unceasing music of these ocean surges rose and fell as now. Moreover, during those unnumbered centuries, day after day, year after year, with ceaseless regularity, the radiance of the setting sun had changed this dark Plutonic passage to a path of gold. Was, then, this glory wasted, when no human eye beheld it? Far from it. Man is not everything upon this planet. The mighty cave of Fingal teaches us this secret of the universe, — that here, as everywhere, in ways unknown to man, the elements pay homage to their Maker. In this way only can we comprehend why countless æons ere a human eye beheld a sunset here, or an ear listened to this ocean symphony, the vast Atlantic thundered its exultant anthem through this majestic minster of the sea.

LOOKING SEAWARD.

ENGLAND

AN ENGLISH LANE.

England

THE greatest benefit to be derived from traveling through this world of ours comes from the proofs of human thought discoverable in the memorials of great achievements. Why does the Rhine appeal to us more powerfully than the Amazon? The European river in respect to size is, by comparison, insignificant; but while the South American stream is well-nigh meaningless, each echo on the other's shores is eloquent of history. Why does the St. Bernard attract us more than others of its Alpine brethren?

QUEEN VICTORIA.

Far loftier peaks environ it. Compared to the Himalayas it is but a pygmy. The secret of its fascination is the fact that Hannibal and Bonaparte have led their legions over it and that, to-day, almost completely isolated from the outer world, heroic monks are living there, risking their lives to rescue travelers from the storm and the avalanche. It is not difficult, therefore, to discover the subtle charm that lures us to "Old England." There is no portion of our globe whose literary and historic souvenirs touch us so profoundly; and we need have no fear that reverence for the Mother Country, inspired by such causes, will be interpreted as Anglomania.

OLD OAK IN THE CENTRE OF ENGLAND.

We could not be identical with the English, even if we would. Although connected by the ties of blood, each nation has its own peculiar character, and its own destiny to work out on the stage of history. This fact is fast becoming recognized. Although they may refrain from saying so, the English are, at heart, proud of our achievements; and we, too, secretly admire "that isle that is itself a world," and which, to-day, controls an area vaster than the empire of the Cæsars. The friction which arises in the intercourse of English and Americans comes chiefly from some insignificant points of difference between us. We are so much alike that both of us, unfortunately, adopt the privilege of relatives and criticise each other. We do not care

AN ENGLISH LANE.

what clothes the Germans or Italians wear, or what may be their intonation and pronunciation, but we are vexed to see our English cousins dress and speak as we do not. They naturally feel the same, but both of us are rapidly becoming wise enough to ignore trivialities, and meet as brothers on the common ground of liberal education, lofty character, and broad ideas of justice and humanity.

Whether we like the English Government or not, nothing can change the fact that England is our old home. The child cannot renounce its mother. It is "Old England" there; it is "New England" here. Up to comparatively recent times her history is also ours. The same words that express their joys and sorrows signify our own. However widely we may drift apart, a common literature grapples us together as with hooks of steel. Shakespeare, Gray, Byron, Dickens, Thackeray, Carlyle, Tennyson, and George Eliot, — of these immortal names we are as proud as Englishmen can ever be.

SHAKESPEARE.

The sentiment which I desire to see increase on both sides of the Atlantic is that which led the English to adorn Westminster Abbey with a bust of Longfellow, and prompted us to place a fine memorial window over the sacred dust of Shakespeare. Old England's literary heroes still outnumber ours, since we are comparatively young, and stern necessity, hitherto, has compelled us to devote our attention to other problems than the development of a national literature; but give us time and, as an American poet has prophesied, our list will be extended. Among his finest lines are those in which he considers from which section of our great republic our future brightest Star of Poesy will rise.

"Perchance the blue Atlantic's brink,
The broad Ohio's gleam,
Or where the panther stoops to drink
Of wild Missouri's stream:

. . . .

Where winter clasps in glittering ice
Katahdin's silver chains,
Or Georgia's flowery paradise
Unfolds its blushing plains.

Be patient! Love hath long been grown,
Ambition waxeth strong,
And Heaven is asking Time alone
To mold our Child of Song."

BUST OF LONGFELLOW IN WESTMINSTER ABBEY.

Who can forget his first glimpse of Old England after an ocean voyage? No matter how many times we have beheld it, it always fills us with surprise, rising so boldly out of the apparently unlimited expanse, through which we have been plowing night and day, a week or more, without a glimpse of anything more solid than the pitching steamer or the rolling waves. How well I recollect my first arrival off the English coast! It was early in the morning, and my bones were in a state of mutiny within a berth which seemed to me a fearful combination of both bed and board. Suddenly a voice in the passageway cried, "Land

THE EDGE OF ENGLAND.

LAND'S-END.

in sight!" I sprang upon the narrow sofa and looked through the port-hole. It was true, the voyage was practically ended; for here was land at last. This was the lighthouse, then, whose friendly flame had welcomed us far out at sea; and from this headland, half an hour before, the news of our arrival had been flashed beneath the mighty ocean we had traversed, so that our friends (strange thought) might read that morning at their breakfast tables the little words which mean so much to them and us (so little to the outside world), "Arrived, the Umbria." All commonplace enough in one sense, it is true, but there is veritable romance in it yet to those who, notwithstanding their advancing years and the stupendous marvels of invention, still keep their hearts young and refuse to be *blasé*.

THE LIGHTHOUSE.

Meantime the news of "land in sight" has had a wonderful effect in bringing unknown passengers to the surface. Pale, sallow creatures have appeared on deck whom we have never seen before, their faces pinched with traces of the woes they have endured. Some cruel travelers ask them when they came aboard. One wretched man, who has existed seven days and nights in the upper berth of an inside cabin, creeps forth from

THE STEAMER'S DECK.

his seclusion like a hermit crab and, in the voice of one far gone in galloping consumption, gives three feeble cheers for England. We soon perceive changes of toilet in our passengers. Men who for seven days have looked like tramps, now shine resplendent in silk hats and glossy broadcloth. Ladies whose hair throughout the voyage has drooped about their heads like seaweed clinging to a rock, now charm us with tight crimps and stylish hats. Nor is this all. Their manners, too, have changed. With new clothes they have grown more dignified, and people who have played upon the deck, like children at the game of shovel-board, now talk with all the stiff propriety of worldly men at a church sociable. Only their noses, parboiled by the sun, shine as reminders of the happy past.

THE "TENDER."

To take us to the pier steams up a boat

sarcastically called a "tender." Tender, indeed! A more appropriate title for it would be "tough," for a more comfortless conveyance rarely rode the waves. I grant in pleasant weather it can be endured; but, oh, what misery to land thus in a rainstorm! This first specimen of England's traveling conveniences has not much roof at best, and but a few hard benches under it; yet here we huddle like "dumb, driven cattle," and wait, wait, wait, until the baggage is brought down from the ship and piled in great confusion all about us. At last, however, the agony is over. The tender starts, some ringing cheers go up for the good steamer and her officers, and we approach the pier.

THE CUSTOM HOUSE PIER, LIVERPOOL.

But now behold us in a kind of pen, like spring lambs ready for the slaughter, waiting again until our baggage is taken to the Custom House. This is perhaps the harder to endure because we know that we have nothing dutiable in our luggage. How sweet is that first consciousness of innocence! We shall not keep it long, nor do we dream of what we shall be capable when once more we land in New York. How our (as yet) untempted souls would here recoil, could we foresee the scores of *Bon Marché* kid gloves which then will lie concealed in coat-sleeves or the legs of trousers; the silks cut up and draped to represent old dresses, and then the presents (oh, those presents!), from jewelry to music-boxes, and perfect bargains from the Printemps and the Magasin du Louvre! Such things must cause us then more mental anguish than twice the money would atone for; since conscience will make cowards of us all.

Finally, emerging from this ordeal, we seat ourselves in a curious equipage, which bears the name of "four-wheeler." Have any new four-wheelers been manufactured during the last twenty years? I should really like to know; for all that I have seen have been back numbers with dilapidated bindings. They are, in general, the shabbiest and most antiquated cabs that ever rattled over cobblestones. The roof seems hardly strong enough to bear a quilt of eider-down; yet on this, with the utmost recklessness, are piled trunks, bundles, and portmanteaus, till our hair stands on end as we creep in below them. When two of us are wedged beneath the threatening avalanche, and two more try to take the opposite seat, a shriek is usually heard, followed by a profuse apology. For time and skill are needed in a cab like this to fit into their proper places eight human legs and feet which, finally, have to interlock like knife-blades, while not a single passenger can move without a

A "FOUR-WHEELER."

CABMEN'S SHELTER.

revolution of the entire company. But, perhaps, some of the party in despair leave this uncomfortable box and seek a hansom. By this invention England has redeemed herself, for hansoms rank, to-day, among the most essential luxuries of city life. We are accustomed now to these models of conciseness, but how astonished was the public when they first appeared! The driver sits upon his perch behind, below which hangs the horse's grain. The passenger steps upon the iron platform, sits down within the pretty cab, closes before him, as a partial screen, the folding doors, and then is driven quickly through the streets with nothing to obstruct his view; while, if he wishes to address the

A HANSOM.

ENGLISH VEHICLES.

coachman, an opening in the roof permits them to converse like Pyramus and Thisbe. What wonder that Lord Beaconsfield poetically called hansoms the "gondolas of the London streets"? Almost all prominent cities of America now possess them; yet it was not long ago that, amid shouts of laughter from the bystanders, an American cow-boy who had never seen a hansom climbed over its closed doors to get inside, and, having there by frightful contortions twisted himself around, considered ruefully how he was ever to get out again.

A TRAM-CAR.

If from the window of one of these vehicles we should behold a horse-car, we might at first mistake it for a private advertising scheme of "Lewis the Tailor," for on all English trams and omnibuses the amount of advertising is so great that it is sometimes difficult to know whether the vehicle is going to Piccadilly or "Mixed Pickles," to Maiden Lane or the "Gaiety Girl." These cars are somewhat like those of American cities, with the exception of an upper story, where those who choose to climb the winding stairs obtain a fine view of the city at small expense. But whether one rides on the inside or the outside of an English tram-car, he is never crowded; for, quite unlike our social way of trampling on one another in public conveyances, each person here has a seat, and when the seats are occupied, no other passengers are admitted.

A RAILWAY STATION.

For elegance and comfort, the drawing-room cars of the United States surpass all others in the world; but there are certain features of English railroad management which might well be adopted everywhere. One is the host of uniformed porters, who spring forth to assist on the arrival of the train, relieving us of bags and parcels; bringing our baggage from the van; calling a cab; assisting us into it with our satchels, and telling the driver our destination: all of which is so quietly and quickly done that, were I asked to name a specimen of almost

AN ENGLISH RAILWAY ENGINE.

perfect service, I should say "that of an English railroad porter."

An English locomotive looks decidedly unfinished; for, instead of our wedge-shaped cow-catcher, we see in front of it merely iron buffers (such as, also, exist at the end of every car), to lessen by huge springs the shock of a collision. How strangely comfortless appears the standing-place for engineer and fireman! With us it is encased with glass and comfortably roofed; but the English stoker is often left to face the elements almost unprotected, being sometimes soaked to the skin and nearly blinded, as he whirls along at fifty miles an hour through the rain or snow.

"Why have you not more shelter from the weather?" I once asked an English stoker.

"Oh, well, Sir," was the reply, "it never 'as been done, Sir; and tho' it's pretty 'ard now and again, Sir, we get along quite well on the 'ole, Sir."

"It never has been done," — that is the secret of many strange discomforts in conservative Old England. Yet we can understand, at least, why English locomotives have no cow-catchers. They would be quite superfluous, since English engines have no chance to catch a cow or, for that matter, any moving obstacle. Throughout the whole of England no railway is allowed to cross a street at grade, and walls or fences keep out all intruders through every mile of its entire length. Moreover, the bridges and embankments, always made of stone, give one a feeling of security, which many railways in America, with their light wooden trestleworks, do not inspire.

Another feature in the English railway system, which sends through the American's soul a thrill of admiration, is the way in which his baggage is there treated. I gazed, at first, in blank astonishment to see my trunk lifted and carried by two men, as if it really had some value, instead of being dropped with a terrific crash upon a platform three or four feet below the baggage-car, or else hurled end over end by some relentless baggage-anarchist. Odd, is it not? England will not check

AN ENGLISH RAILWAY.

baggage; America will not take proper care of it. In the one country it is often getting lost; in the other it is as often getting smashed.

It was on a beautiful afternoon in May, soon after my first landing in Liverpool, that I caught sight of the old town of Chester on the river Dee. In the immediate foreground was a massive bridge built, by King Edward I., two hundred years before Columbus gazed upon the shores of the New World. As I look back upon it now, through a long vista lined with the more ancient monuments of Italy, Asia Minor, India, and Egypt, I wonder at the impression which this structure made upon me. But it was my first sight, then, of any genuine relic of past centuries; and the mere thought that these old arches had supported Queen Elizabeth, Charles I., Cromwell, and scores of other royal or distinguished characters gave me my first experience in *realizing history*, which is, perhaps, the greatest charm of foreign travel. But these impressions sank into comparative insignificance as, on our way to the hotel, we passed an ancient tower, carefully restored. Beside this monument, even the bridge of Edward I. seemed modern; since this once formed a part of the old walls of Chester, and its founda-

OLD BRIDGE AT CHESTER.

CHESTER CATHEDRAL.

OLD INN AT CHESTER.

tions are a relic of imperial Rome. Chester was, in fact, for four hundred years, a Roman stronghold of such value that, as its name denotes, it was called simply *Castrum*, or "The Camp," — much as old Rome herself was proudly named, as if that single title were sufficient, *Urbs*, "The City." We cannot, therefore, be surprised to learn that in its soil coins, inscriptions, altars, and mosaic pavements have been found, all dating from the time when a word uttered on the Palatine was obeyed in Britain, and Rome was still the mistress of the world.

I know of nothing precisely like the walls of Chester. The Kremlin battlements in Moscow may suggest them; but the old Russian towers have summits almost inaccessible, while

A PART OF THE OLD WALL, CHESTER.

KING CHARLES' TOWER.

these thick walls of Chester enclose the town in one continuous ring, and form a well-paved promenade, nearly two miles in circuit and in some places forty feet in height. How stirring are the memories which they suggest! Here, for centuries, while the young Christian Church with tears and prayers was burying its martyrs in the catacombs, the soldiers of the Cæsars kept their watch and ward above the town below, till the eventful day when Rome's imperial legions were called back to Italy, to ward off the alarming blows struck by barbarians at the Empire's heart. Upon the surface of one of these turrets, also, I read the inscription: "Upon this tower, Sept. 27, 1645, stood King Charles I., and saw his army defeated on Rowton Moor." For Chester ("loyal Chester," it was then called) was the first English city to declare for Charles, and

OLD CHESTER HOUSES.

WATERGATE ROW, CHESTER.

the last to yield to Cromwell; and it was with the bitter consciousness that the last gem was being taken from his coronet of faithful towns, that the unhappy monarch (himself so soon to suffer death) saw from this tower his gallant cavaliers borne down by the fierce squadrons of the Puritans.

I never saw more curious architecture, even in the oldest towns of Germany, than that of some of Chester's streets. A score of times I said, regretfully, "Why did not Dickens give to these odd passageways some of his inimitable descriptions?" He, of all writers, would have fairly reveled here. Thus, some of the houses have to lean against their neighbors for support, as if too weak to stand alone, or out of breath from their long race with Time. Their very foundations seem to have shrunk away, like the limbs of a paralytic, and look as if they might collapse at any moment and let the superstructure fall.

Still more extraordinary than these, however, are Chester's covered sidewalks. Their sombre hue and well-worn steps attest their great antiquity, and it is interesting to learn that they are supposed to follow exactly the lines of the original Roman thoroughfares. They are called "Rows," but certainly not because of any perfume here of Jacqueminots. By any name they would smell no more sweetly; for musty odors haunt these low-browed corridors, and damp, unsavory smells creep out from the old planks and flagstones never gilded by the sun. Yet in these shadowy arcades are many handsome shops, above which frequently dwell the tradesmen's families. One of the houses surmounting these sidewalks has a more juvenile appearance than its neighbors, since it was reconstructed thirty years ago. Upon the sill, however, just above the corridor, I read the ancient inscription: "God's Providence is my inheritance." Is it possible that these words betray the owner's disappointment on coming into possession of this residence? Apparently he had more faith in Providence than in the value of the premises. I fancy that his sentiments must have been, "God only knows what I am going to realize from this property." A friend of mine, who had invested heavily in Western farm mortgages here turned his face to the wall and wiped away a tear. It is claimed, however, that this inscription denotes the owner's gratitude to Providence for having spared his dwelling

THE "RECONSTRUCTED" HOUSE.

ROMAN WALL IN ENGLAND.

during the ravages of the plague in Chester two hundred years ago.

Chester is not the only place in England that has Roman relics. In many portions of the island we come upon walls that once surrounded Roman camps. It is indeed a curious fact that almost all the traces of the Cæsars in Great Britain are military in their character. The Roman occupation was not long enough to allow great cities, aqueducts, and amphitheatres to be built here, as in Gaul and Spain. The legionaries of the Empire did, however, construct a wall twelve feet in height and eight in thickness which stretched across the north of England, from the Atlantic to the North Sea, to protect England from the barbarous tribes of Scotland.

GROSVENOR BRIDGE, NEAR CHESTER.

ELY CATHEDRAL.

To appreciate the magnitude of this achievement, it should be remembered that it was a rampart seventy-five miles long, with a deep, broad ditch before it; and that this barricade was garrisoned by Roman cohorts, lodged in forts a mile apart from one another, between which, nevertheless, were numerous watch-towers; while at every four miles was a military station covering several acres.

Traveling on from Chester into the open country, I soon began to realize how full of interest English landscapes always are. In England attractive objects crowd on one another. There can be no monotony. The theatre is too small. There is no room to spare. Both men and things are stowed away compactly. The traveler's attention is, therefore, kept continually alert. The panoramic stage of England never waits. One travels here as he assists at a continuous performance, with the stupendous climax, London, at the end.

Sometimes, in looking from the window of his railway carriage, the tourist sees the fluted towers of an old cathedral, as stately and imposing as the battlements of a Norman castle. England is proud of her cathedrals, and her inhabitants gladly tax themselves to keep them in repair. Perhaps, comparatively few of those who thus support them worship there. They may prefer their individual parishes, or may be Dissenters from the Church of England; but they regard these grand old minsters as priceless illustrations of their national life, which must not be destroyed. In fact, how different English history must seem to children or adults, who study it amid such surroundings, looking upon creations of inspired art, touching the relics of past centuries, and standing by the graves of those whom history records!

No one can travel far in England without observing with delight its universal verdure. This cannot be too highly praised. When other lands are white with dust, the fields of England are fresh and moist, and all its wealth of foliage is undimmed. In summer the entire island seems to be covered

ENGLISH VERDURE.

with a beautiful green carpet, of which the hedges, trees, and flowers are the figured patterns. The very walls are cushioned with soft turf; the rustic houses veil themselves with vines; wild roses twine above the porches, and honeysuckles climb adventurously to the eaves. Truly the fogs of London are abundantly atoned for by the rural beauty of this island gem.

Farming in England is done on so small a scale that to a laborer on the western prairies of the United States it would seem absurd; yet nowhere in the world does harvesting present a prettier picture. Almost all English landscapes seem to have been finished with a brush and pencil, and even the hillsides look well-groomed. There are no lofty mountains; for, as Mrs. Browning said,

> "God's finger touched, but did not press,
> In making England";

but Britain's beautifully rounded slopes and the perpetual verdure of its fields harmonize perfectly with the subdued light that filters through its customary canopy of clouds. We must console ourselves for frequent showers here, since it is England's copious rain that renders it thus fresh and green, and makes of it the garden of the world. It is not strange, then, that where such results can be obtained from moisture, Englishmen often prefer the clouds of their own island to the clear skies of southern Europe. "These blue Italian skies are well

FARMING IN ENGLAND.

THE IZAAK WALTON INN, DOVEDALE.

enough in theory," a Briton once exclaimed, "but their incessant glare oppresses me. I want moisture," he continued, "I want rain; yes," he added, with a tender emphasis, "nice, warm, muggy rain."

A ROSE-COVERED COTTAGE.

Another glory of the Mother Country is her trees. Ideal specimens of them greet us everywhere, looking as sturdy as the race they shelter, yet often as symmetrical as if produced by art. They usually stand alone in isolated majesty; and even when they seem to be in groups, they still maintain a cold reserve and distance from their fellows, suggestive of the men who planted them. The German Empire has more extensive forests than Old England, and we on our Pacific slope possess arboreal giants of much larger growth; but in no country in the world that

AN ENGLISH OAK.

I have ever visited, save, possibly, our own Connecticut valley, do noble oaks and elms form such a frequent and delightful feature of the landscape as in England.

Another charm of English scenery is the finished, well-kept character of everything we see. The fences are not made of zigzag rails, nor yet of stumps of trees, which sometimes in America's rural districts line the roads for miles, like the extracted teeth of prehistoric monsters. The English fields are usually framed with hedges; the roads are neat and tasteful as a garden walk; and winding lanes, all bright with flowers, constitute ideal walks for lovers. There are no traces here of hasty growth, and we perceive at last that all this rustic loveliness is the result of centuries of civilization. Whether an energetic young American would like to live in such a fixed environment is one thing, but certainly to an American traveler it is both novel and delightful.

What can be prettier and more picturesque than one of the quaint old English inns, which Dickens and a score of other writers have described? Some years ago these little hostelries

A WELL-KEPT AVENUE.

AN ENGLISH INN.

maintained themselves with difficulty. The substitution of the railroad for the stage-coach had given them, apparently, a fatal blow; but with the advent of the bicycle they are reviving. Aside from the English, themselves, the number of Americans who ride through England every summer now is astonishing. England is indeed a paradise for bicyclists. The roads are admirably made; the distances between attractive halting-places are short; the climate is cooler than our own; the cost of such travel is comparatively small; and all along the way the wheelman comes upon little inns where he can rest and take a modest lunch, or pass the night, certain of cleanliness at least to compensate him for the homely fare.

One of the first excursions that I made in England was to Stonehenge, on the Salisbury Plain. As I approached the place, I recognized from a considerable distance its famous group of tall, dark stones rising in bold relief against the sky. Rough and unshapely though they are, I gazed upon them with the deepest interest; for they have been standing here two thousand years, and were undoubtedly marked with age before the founder of Christianity was born. What makes them even more impressive is the mysterious silence that broods over them. Though situated in the very heart of England, the busy world has always kept aloof from them. No voice disturbs the stillness of the broad plateau on which they stand. No rudely carved inscription vaguely tells their secret. Their unrecorded meaning reaches back into the shadows of conjectured history. They were originally placed in couples, and bore aloft a third great monolith, well-nigh as ponderous as themselves. Around them, scattered over the adjoining plain, are the remains of mounds containing funeral urns and weapons of the dead. This area, therefore, was no doubt a burial place for British kings;

STONEHENGE.

"LIKE A COLOSSAL SUN-DIAL."

and these huge blocks once formed a sacred temple of the Druids, that strange and powerful priesthood of the British race. One of these Druidical stones rises in isolation from its comrades, like a colossal sun-dial, whose shadow has been moving on its slow, unchanging path, while kingdoms, dynasties, and even races have flourished here and passed away. If the old monolith could speak, what stories might it tell of the dark days when human sacrifices stained this area with blood! Throughout the Roman occupation, during the night of the Dark Ages, through the slow rise and progress of Christianity, and, finally, through all the power and fame of modern England, this rough-hewn column has looked grimly down upon the plain, as on a stage upon which countless kings and warriors have made their entrances and exits, ephemeral actors in an endless play.

A GIGANTIC TRIO.

Another episode of English travel which I recall with

the greatest pleasure is a visit to the churchyard of Stoke Pogis, to which Gray's matchless "Elegy" has given an undying charm. It has changed little since the poet's time, save that the "ivy-mantled tower" which he described is now surmounted by a modern spire. The latter is not a pleasing addition, and even the ivy, which clings so lovingly to the old walls, avoids the spire as if it were a strange intruder. With this exception, however, the place is as it was when Gray was wont to linger here at sunset, while "the curfew tolled the knell of parting day." Beneath the oriel window, rich with verdure, is the poet's grave, — an ideal resting-place for one who has identified his name forever with its peaceful beauty. I found the poet's home, not far from the church, to be a pretty little cottage, set in a frame of ivy, foliage, and flowers, and embellished, also, by the garden where he often sat elaborating his immortal poem.

STOKE POGIS CHURCHYARD.

GRAY'S GARDEN AND HOUSE.

Gray wrote very carefully and slowly. I once supposed that he composed the "Elegy" in one brief hour of special inspiration in the churchyard; but in reality he labored seven years upon it, till it became a flawless gem of English literature. There is, in my opinion, no poem in the English language every line of which will bear such careful scrutiny; and it is pleasant to repeat it slowly, and to observe how every word, and, in particular, every adjective (which is, of course, the supreme test of all descriptive writing), fits into its place as perfectly as a piece of Florentine mosaic.

Perhaps the best way to explore the central part of England is to establish one's headquarters in the tranquil old town of Leamington. It is not of itself especially attractive, save for its rare good fortune in

GRAY'S MONUMENT, STOKE POGIS.

AN ENGLISH COUNTRY ROAD.

forming the centre of a charming circle, since around it, within easy distances, are some of the most interesting objects in Great Britain. The roads which radiate from Leamington to all these points are perfect, and one can easily walk or drive thence in a few hours to Warwick Castle, Coventry, Kenilworth, and Stratford-on-Avon, or go and return by rail in a day to Oxford, Birmingham, or Manchester.

Few tourists in England fail to visit the finest specimen of feudal architecture in the Queen's dominions, — Warwick Castle. I found the approach to it to be a winding avenue, cut for some distance through the solid rock, on which, however, no roughness was dis-

AN AVENUE AT WARWICK.

cernible, for its sides were almost hidden by a tapestry of ivy. Above it noble trees had interlaced their arms like bosom friends and cast upon the path below a tremulous mosaic of light and shade. At length a sudden turn revealed the castle. It is a sight to thrill the most prosaic traveler. It seemed to me the very ideal of chivalry and poetry crystalized in stone, not merely on account of its architectural beauty, but from the fact that this first glimpse of Warwick placed before

WARWICK CASTLE.

me in a concrete form something which had been dear to me ever since the days when I had followed breathlessly the fascinating stories of "Kenilworth" and "Ivanhoe." It called to mind so vividly the age of gallant knights and brave crusaders that I should hardly have been surprised if I had encountered here some horseman clad in suit of mail, leading his armed retainers forth to render service to his king. Many a time have Warwick's chieftains done this. Some of the trees which cast their shadows in the park are genuine descendants of the cedars of Mt. Lebanon, the seeds of which were brought back from the Holy Land by one of Warwick's earls, who was as brave a knight as ever carried lance in rest or fought the Saracen in Palestine. England has hardly a distinguished office on her list that has not been at times held by members of this noble family. One easily understands, in such a place, the law of primogeniture, and comprehends how an old family estate, with its inherited beauty, history, and traditions, should never be divided up and thus eventually lost.

On one of the ivied towers of Warwick Castle, as if to emphasize the fact of its antiquity, is an ancient sun-dial, which tells to us the same impressive story that it told to the lords and ladies who rode beneath it centuries ago, — that of the constant and irrevocable flight of Time. No motto is inscribed beneath it; but it recalled to me some words which, when I read them round a sun-dial in Spain, seemed strikingly appro-

THE CEDARS OF MT. LEBANON, WARWICK CASTLE.

THE SUN-DIAL TOWER,
AND THE COURTYARD.

priate, as applied to the passing moments of life: "They all wound; the last kills!" Strolling onward from this gate, we gained a better view of the great court, where knightly tournaments frequently took place in view of England's King, or Queen, and the fairest ladies of the realm. Yet, in striking contrast to this sunlit area, beneath one of the adjoining towers, is a dismal dungeon within which, doubtless, many a prisoner languished — possibly died — while echoes of the joyous sports were borne to him upon the breeze. Little is known of those captives; but they, at least, were human beings like ourselves, with friends who loved them, and whom they loved in turn; and in the gloomy vault may still be seen their names, initials, or a word of prayer traced in the stone by the poor victims who thus appealed from tyranny to God.

The grand reception-hall of Warwick Castle must have been a magnificent assembling place for kings and warriors of the

THE RECEPTION-HALL.

past, as it is for lords and ladies of the present time. Around the walls are battle-axes, spears, and suits of armor, once used or worn by members of the family in feudal times; but now they are all tenantless. The valiant hearts that beat beneath them are forever stilled. The hands that wielded these enormous weapons have crumbled to decay.

> "Their swords are rust:
> Their bones are dust:
> Their souls are with the saints, we trust."

In other apartments of the castle the wealth of centuries seems to have been gathered. Rare ornaments in bronze or marble stand upon tables of mosaic, or pedestals of lapis-lazuli.

THE DRAWING-ROOM.

A STREET IN WARWICK.

Upon the walls hang paintings by Vandyke and Rubens; and Henry VIII., Charles I., Queen Anne, and Oliver Cromwell look down upon us from their gilded frames, and seem to mock us with their changeless scrutiny and their red lips that never speak. If it were not too fanciful, one might query here whether they ever do converse after the guests are gone, and if they do not laugh at us who so intently study their careers, and think we understand the motives which inspired them. How much less they, when living, knew than we; but, dead, ah, how much more!

LEICESTER'S TOMB IN BEAUCHAMP CHAPEL.

From the rooms where Warwick's chiefs had lived, we passed to the place where some of them lie buried. The chapel is superbly decorated. The walls and ceiling are of elegantly carved oak, and the stained glass windows are aflame with color. Through them, as through the ruby and golden tints of autumn leaves, the sunlight streams upon the upturned faces of the sculptured dead. Clad in full armor, they lie side by side, their joined hands raised as if imploring mercy on their sinful souls. It was an attitude they probably seldom took in life; hence it provokes a smile to see it now obligatory and unchanging. For three long centuries within this chapel has reposed the handsome Earl of Leicester, the favorite of Queen Elizabeth, and one of the most successful triflers with women's hearts this world has ever seen. Yet, in the case of Elizabeth, at least, he certainly received his punishment. Forever on the threshold of the throne he never reached it. Elizabeth played with him as he had done with others. It was a case of royal coquetry in which Elizabeth triumphed; for, unlike her fair cousin, Mary, Queen of Scots, Elizabeth's head always controlled her heart. The picture of her love affairs is, therefore, not particularly brilliant. As the French say, "Flirtation is merely love in water colors."

GUY'S TOWER, WARWICK.

Saying farewell, at last, to Warwick we drove one afternoon to what must certainly be called the loveliest of England's ruined castles, — Kenilworth. The sun was sinking in the west as we rode up the avenue leading thither, and in the radiance of that sunset light the ruined walls and towers glowed like shafts of jasper, resembling the volcanic cliffs of Capri. At first I could not comprehend this marvelous effect, but presently the secret was disclosed; for, to my great astonishment, I discovered that the castle was not gray, but red; composed, in fact, of old red sandstone. No one had ever told me this, and I had formed the idea that its walls were made of granite.

KENILWORTH CASTLE.

I think we naturally expect all ruins to be gray. We ourselves certainly grow gray with time. Why should old castles be more fortunate? Hence, though I finally came to admire the ruddy hue of Kenilworth, it took some time for me to harmonize reality with expectation.

Kenilworth in its prime was far superior to Warwick. Its outer wall enclosed a space of seven acres; ten thousand soldiers were required to guard it; and Elizabeth's fascinating suitor, Leicester, to whom she had presented it, expended on its decorations nearly half a million dollars. Imposing and magnificent it must have been when Leicester gave his entertainments in the famous banquet-hall; for then, as a historian of the time declares, its hundreds of illumined windows blazed like the ancient Alexandrine Pharos, which rose resplendent from the coast of Egypt. Even now, though utterly dismantled by the troops of Cromwell, it is still beautiful; while the historic memories of a place owned by a royal favorite, and visited not only by Queen Elizabeth, but, no doubt, scores of times by Shakespeare from his neighboring town, appeal to us more powerfully than those of any other castle in Old England.

RUINS OF KENILWORTH CASTLE.

One day, in the early part of the present century, a stranger visited these ruins, asked many questions in regard to them, and was seen for several hours walking about and taking notes of all that he observed. He spoke with a broad Scotch accent, and limped a little as he walked. When he was gone the guardian looked at the Visitors' Book to find who he might be. His curiosity was gratified; for the stranger was none other than Sir Walter Scott, who subsequently wrote the novel "Kenilworth," which will, perhaps, be read by generations yet unborn, when the old castle's towers shall have crumbled into dust.

PART OF THE BANQUET-HALL, KENILWORTH.

As we compare the buildings of the past and present, it is a partial consolation for the fact that such magnificent abodes as Kenilworth are now ruins that, even in the period of their glory, they must have been lacking in a multitude of comforts, which we now deem essential to our happiness.

"O, the pleasant days of old, which so often people praise!
True, they wanted all the luxuries that grace our modern days;
Bare floors were strewed with rushes, the walls let in the cold;
O, how they must have shivered in those pleasant days of old!

O, the gentle dames of old! who, quite free from fear or pain,
Could gaze on joist and tournament and see their champions slain;
They lived on good beefsteaks and ale, which made them strong and bold,—
O, more like men than women were those gentle dames of old!

O, those mighty towers of old! with their turrets, moat and keep,
Their battlements and bastions, their dungeons dark and deep.
Full many a baron held his court within the castle bold;
And many a captive languished there, in those strong towers of old!

O, those blessèd times of old, with their chivalry and state!
I love to read their chronicles, which such brave deeds relate;
I love to sing their ancient rhymes, to hear their legends told, —
But, Heaven be thanked! I live not in those blessèd times of old!"

Within the lovely section of England which includes both Kenilworth and Warwick is another spot precious to every English-speaking traveler, — Stratford-on-Avon, the home of Shakespeare. On entering the town Americans usually put up at the "Red Horse Hotel." To lodge elsewhere would seem to them almost unpatriotic, since it was here that Washington Irving resided during his stay in Stratford, nearly seventy years ago; and here he wrote those exquisite reflections, which still attract us to the charming pages of his "Sketch Book." The room which Irving occupied is now kept conse-

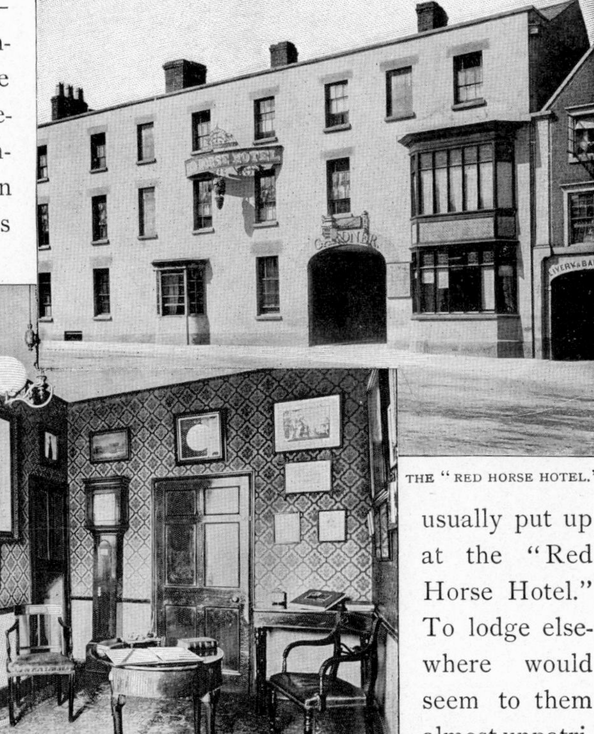

THE "RED HORSE HOTEL."

WASHINGTON IRVING'S ROOM.

SHAKESPEARE'S HOUSE.

crated to his memory, and the mahogany arm-chair in which the author sat on the memorable evening he has described is distinguished by a brass plate bearing his name. Beside it, within easy reach, is also placed the poker which Irving playfully called his "sceptre," since with this, as with a magic wand, he fancied that he ruled that night the spirits of the mighty dead, and called them up before him at his will. It is appropriate, therefore, that upon its side, in finely engraved characters, are the words: "Geoffrey Crayon's Sceptre." A score of photographs had made the house of Shakespeare so familiar to me for years that I was hardly prepared for the wave of feeling that rolled over me when I beheld the actual building in which the grandest poet of the world first saw the light. A calmer, closer scrutiny, however, made the exterior of the house seem disappointing. Its walls have been so frequently and carefully restored that its real age appears almost incredible. Nor is it in itself attractive. It fronts upon the street. No shade trees are around it. No avenue leads up to it. No garden gives to it the least retirement. One feels that, if young Shakespeare could have been consulted, he would have chosen a different birthplace.

The room in which the dramatist was born is low and ugly in appearance, yet what apartment in the most magnificent palace is of such value to the human race! I found it difficult, however, to think of Shakespeare as a child amid these surroundings. The tread of millions has replaced the echoes of his childish feet; the walls and even the ceiling are so thickly covered with the names of visitors that the apartment has become a roughly bound collection of illustrious autographs; and Shakespeare's spirit seems to have departed from the place, like the bright fire that once gleamed upon the hearth, beside which the young poet and his mother used to sit, unconscious of his mighty destiny.

ROOM WHERE SHAKESPEARE WAS BORN.

A portrait of the immortal bard is here exhibited, but I have never met a traveler who liked it, or who could quite persuade himself that it bears much resemblance to the author of "Hamlet" and "Othello." But what reputed likeness ever could do justice to our ideal of this sublime interpreter of human nature? No single cast of features seems appropriate to one whose genius was so universal. Instinctively we feel that Shakespeare's face should be as varied in expression as his mind: assuming now the cunning of Iago, and now the sweetness of Ophelia; the wild hilarity of Petruchio, the innocence of Cymbeline; the low buffoonery of Falstaff, or the thoughtfulness of Hamlet. Truly, if only arduous study and exceptional genius can portray their characters, what likeness can depict, as we imagine him, their versatile and unsurpassed creator?

PORTRAIT OF SHAKESPEARE.

What brought me nearest to the personality of Shakespeare was a short walk across the fields to the quaint, thatch-roofed cottage of his wife, Anne Hathaway. It was the hour of sunset as I lingered here, and nightingales and thrushes were singing in the elms and hedges, as sweetly, doubtless, as they did when Shakespeare whispered to Anne Hathaway the story of his love. What an incomparable suitor must he have been who has given to the world that most adorable of lovers, Romeo! Whatever

STRATFORD-ON-AVON.

may be said about great geniuses making poor husbands, there can be little question of their fascination in those delightful hours of uncertainty and novelty, known as courtship and the honeymoon. Anne Hathaway's cottage is a characteristic farm-house of the reign of Queen Elizabeth, and even apart from its historical associations would be interesting; but with what reverence we step upon its old stone floor, when we remember it has echoed to the tread of Shakespeare! Into its fireplace his glorious eyes have, no doubt, gazed, and on the uncouth, time-worn bench which stands there still, he often sat beside the woman whom he wooed and won. The very timbers in the ceiling, visible to-day, have heard his whispers of impassioned love. What words they must have been, we can imagine from the experiences of Portia, Rosalind, and Juliet. One stands here lost in wondering what sort of a woman this Anne Hathaway was, whom this incomparable genius loved and married, who was the mother of his children, and whom he lived with con-

ANNE HATHAWAY'S COTTAGE.

THE INTERIOR OF ANNE HATHAWAY'S COTTAGE.

stantly, until obliged to go away to London to seek fame and fortune. As then, emerging from the cottage, I took my farewell of its picturesque, flower-laden walls, I kept repeating to myself the stanzas, in which the enamoured poet is said to have addressed the nightingales and thrushes in these very fields:

> "Would ye be taught, ye feathered throng,
> With love's sweet notes to grace your song,
> To pierce the heart with thrilling lay,
> Listen to mine Anne Hathaway!
> She hath a way to sing so clear,
> Phœbus might wondering stop to hear.
> To melt the sad, make blithe the gay,
> And nature charm, Anne hath a way;
> She hath a way,
> Anne Hathaway,
> To breathe delight Anne hath a way."

Leaving at last this interesting cottage, I made my way to the beautiful old church of Stratford, which, standing in the shade of ancient elms, and with the silvery Avon slipping by its walls, is almost ideal in its peaceful beauty. It was a perfect day when I approached it. The paths were flecked with sunlight, filtering through the trees; and as I leaned upon the ivied wall, and looked across the quaint old tombstones toward the open door, I heard the music of the organ, now rising in well-rounded harmony, now sinking into dreamy melody, above which rose the murmur of the Avon at my feet.

"Is there a service going on?" I asked of the old sexton.

"O, no, Sir," he replied, "the organist is only practicing. You may go in, Sir, if you like."

Accordingly I crossed the churchyard — which seemed almost too beautiful to leave — and stepped within the sacred edifice. I do not recollect a more impressive moment in my life. This is indeed a place thrice hallowed: first, by its dedication to Almighty God; secondly, by the priceless dust which it contains; and, thirdly, by the universal reverence of mankind. Here one believes and must believe in immortality.

TRINITY CHURCH, STRATFORD-ON-AVON

What! shall such intellect as that of Shakespeare dissolve to nothingness like an extinguished flame? Impossible. Great genius is a connecting link between man and God. The walls of this old church contain some beautiful memorial windows; but, ere I could bestow a glance on them, my gaze was drawn, as by a magnet, to a marble bust set in a sculptured frame. Below it was a large flat stone. I walked slowly on till I stood beside it, and on its surface read the well-known lines:

"Good Friend, for Jesus' sake forbear
To dig the dust enclosèd here.
Blest be the man that spares these stones,
And curst be he that moves my bones."

For three long centuries this epitaph has guarded Shakespeare's sepulchre, like the destroying angel's sword of flame. Protected by that awful imprecation the Bard of Avon has slept undisturbed. At first I could not understand why the writer of the grand soliloquy of "Hamlet" should not have ordered for his tomb a nobler sentiment than this. One from a thousand of his well-known lines on death, or immortality, or that "undiscovered country, from whose bourne no traveler returns," would have been more appropriate to his majestic intellect; but Death,

INTERIOR OF TRINITY CHURCH.

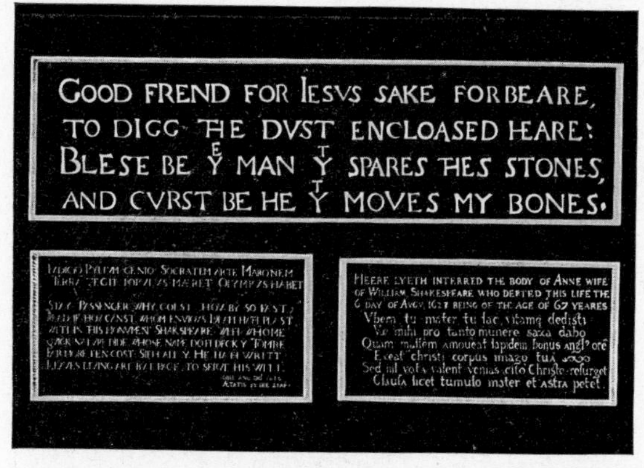

THE EPITAPH.

when looked upon and described poetically, is very different from the Death that summons us to follow him. Before the first, one may be philosophic; before the second, he is practical. World-weary, weak, and longing for repose, the poet then becomes again the man.

A remarkable proof that Shakespeare's mighty spirit was never more potent than it is at the present time is the Shakespeare Memorial, completed here in 1880. It is a combination of theatre, library, and museum, forever dedicated to the man whose name it bears; and on its stage Shakespearean plays are annually presented by gifted artists of the English-speaking race. Americans appear in them as well as English. Within its walls, for example, Mary Anderson has acted, assuming here for the first time the character of Rosalind, and she is, to-day, one of the

THE SHAKESPEARE MEMORIAL.

THE SHAKESPEARE LIBRARY.

directors of the institution; while among the first contributors to the memorial fund which made this building possible, was Edwin Booth. Within its library are more than six thousand books on Shakespeare, written in various languages, and here are, also, most of the editions of his plays.

American tourists in Stratford note with interest the memorial fountain, presented to the town, in 1887, by the munificent citizen of Philadelphia, George W. Childs. At its dedication the English actor, Sir Henry Irving, delivered an address, and read a poem, written for the occasion by Oliver Wendell Holmes. It is a handsome structure, the utility of which is proved by the stream of water which flows continually into a polished granite basin;

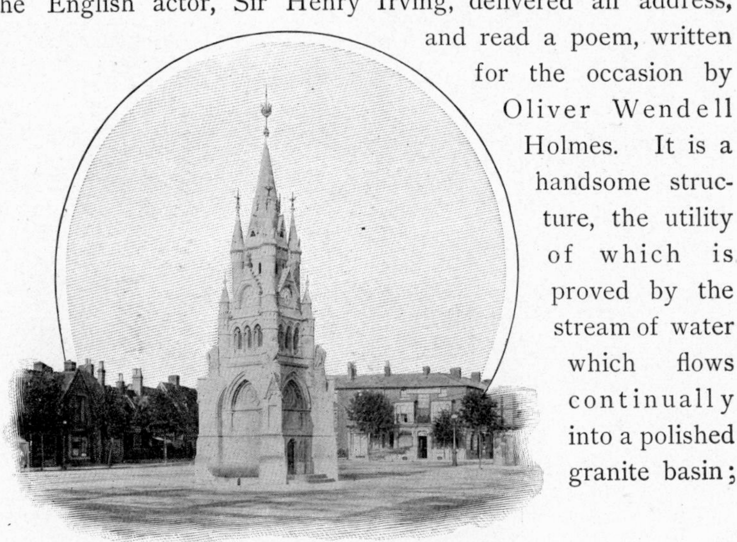

THE CHILDS FOUNTAIN.

while among its Gothic towers is a clock, whose deep-toned voice proclaims the passing hours to a town that will be world-renowned while Time endures.

Leaving this bond of union between England and America, I strolled beside the river Avon, which, like a silver ribbon, threads its way for miles between green meadows carpeted with velvet turf and gemmed with flowers. The very trees seem fond of this historic stream; for they bend over it, gaze into

BESIDE THE AVON.

its dark depths, and with their countless fingers touch caressingly its limpid waves. Surely, beside this stream of Shakespeare all national differences can be forgotten. Upon the Avon's banks Americans and English form but one historic family, bowing alike in filial admiration for the king of poets, and claiming as their common heritage the noble English language, which the great bard of Stratford has so glorified.

One of the most enjoyable excursions I ever made in England had for its destination the historic mansion known as Haddon Hall. The grounds of this estate possess an endless charm, being built up in stately terraces, with long-drawn paths and massive balustrades, above which grand old English oaks spread out their agèd but protecting arms. It would be difficult to imagine a more delightful country-seat than this, possessing, as it does, extensive area and boundless shade, as well as numberless historic memories. For Haddon Hall has been in existence more than seven hundred years, and during all that time has been in the possession of only two families. As, therefore, I descended from one flower-bordered staircase to another, the Muse of History seemed lurking in the shadows of this sylvan solitude, and I could fancy that the ghosts of former actors on this stage were silently awaiting me at the dark terminus of every avenue. In fact, so laden is the atmosphere of Haddon with romantic legends, that one half expects to meet here some of the former occupants of the place, arrayed in velvets, silks, and jewels, and eagerly discussing the exciting news of the defeat of the Armada, or the escape of

HADDON HALL, FROM THE RIVER.

DOROTHY VERNON'S WALK.

Mary, Queen of Scots. It was, however, on the upper terrace that we were told of Haddon's most romantic bit of history.

"That," said our guide, "is Dorothy Vernon's door."

"And who was Dorothy Vernon?" we inquired.

The old man looked a little shocked, and then replied: "Miss Dorothy, Sir, was the fairest woman of all who were ever christened, married, or buried from Haddon Hall. That," he continued, "was in 1567, when Dorothy's father, Sir George Vernon, lived here in such style that he was famed throughout all England for his princely hospitality."

THE BANQUET-HALL.

"Was Dorothy the only daughter?" we asked.

"No, there were two of them," was the

reply, "and it was on the very night when her elder sister, Margaret, had been married here that through this door and down these steps fair Mistress Dorothy eloped."

"Eloped?" we cried; "this promises to be exciting. Go on."

The old attendant warmed up like an actor under generous applause, and led us into the ball-room of the castle. "Well," he exclaimed, with the alacrity and earnestness of one who told the facts for the first time, "it happened thus: the wedding guests had come hither from the chapel, when it was suddenly perceived that Mistress Dorothy had disappeared. No one could fail to notice this; for she was far more beautiful than any other lady at the ball, and was fairly idolized by all who knew her. None of her many suitors had pleased her, except one handsome fellow, named John Manners, son of the Earl of Rutland. Against him no objection could be urged, save that of a long-existing family quarrel. But over such a barrier the lovers thought that they could safely leap. Yes, come to this window," he continued, "and you will see down there, among the trees, a little structure still called 'Dorothy Vernon's Bridge.' Close by this, hidden in the shade, that night, stood Dorothy's lover, young John Manners, who had not been invited to the ball. Meantime, a mutual friend, while dancing with Miss Dorothy, whispered a message from her

DOROTHY VERNON'S STEPS.

HADDON HALL.

lover, and in a moment more the girl had left the room, and, hastening across that bridge, was instantly encircled by her lover's arms. Horses were waiting a few yards away, and off they rode through the summer night, and the next morning, in Leicestershire, were made man and wife. John Manners was, indeed, doubly fortunate; for he not only won a beautiful bride, but, after a short time, the whole estate of Haddon Hall passed by this marriage into the possession of his family, by whom it has been held more than three hundred years."

DOROTHY VERNON'S FOOTBRIDGE.

In listening to this story, I could but think how "Love will find the way" in every age and land. He is a wonderful god; his kingdom reaches to the farthest boundaries of humanity; his altar rises in every heart; his litanies are chanted in every tongue; and his sacrifices, ah! where are they not found! His magic power transmutes every substance; glorifies every thought; deifies the loved one; and, when his potency is absolutely felt, it is as hopeless to resist him as to eliminate the sun from the universe by a breath, or to destroy the pyramids by a stroke of the hand. How perfect would his sovereignty be, were it always changeless and immortal! But, alas! how seldom do lovers see the realization of their beautiful ideal of lifelong constancy, and the fulfillment of their wish to pass hand in hand into the sunset of life, and to be together when the night shall fall!

Great centres of instruction and established armories of intellectual weapons have always had a fascination for scholastic minds, from the classic shades of Heliopolis and Plato's Academy to those of fair Harvard and its New World rivals. Hence, for those who have received a classical education and have adopted a professional or literary, rather than a commercial career, the two old University towns of England have a special charm. Stately in architecture, beautiful in their surroundings, and royally endowed with centuries of precious memories, they often lure American travelers to their precincts at the very outset of an English tour. Even apart from their literary associations, Oxford and Cambridge are impressive in their age and history. It is certain that in the former town King Alfred lived, a thousand years ago, and that before his time it was renowned as the seat of a monastery, founded in the eighth century. William the Conqueror built castles in both places; and at Oxford, which Henry II. made his residence for the greater part of his reign, Richard the Lion-hearted was born. Here, too, the visitor may see a time-worn building, known as the "Crown Inn," where Shakespeare used to spend the night when journeying between Stratford and London.

JESUS COLLEGE, OXFORD.

OXFORD.

GATEWAY TO NEW COLLEGE, OXFORD.

It is, however, the educational prominence of these towns for seven hundred years that explains their present influence over the minds of men. For centuries they held the sacred fire of learning, at which were kindled the individual torches of intelligence throughout the kingdom. Even in Chaucer's time these Universities were already old, and Erasmus came from Germany four hundred years ago to study in them. Twenty-four colleges are scattered over the ancient town of Oxford, and nearly as many lend dignity to Cambridge, all beautiful with cloistered courtyards, crenelated walls, innumerable gables, and sculptured windows holding multicolored panes of emerald, amethyst, and gold. What a historic background these old colleges possess! Thus,

ST. EDMUND'S HALL, OXFORD.

St. Edmund's Hall, at Oxford, dates from 1226; "Balliol," in front of which the reformers Latimer, Ridley, and Cranmer were burned, was founded in 1263; even the institution known as New College was established as long ago as 1386; Jesus College was founded by Queen Elizabeth; and "Christ Church" was endowed by Cardinal Wolsey in 1525. The origin of these separate corporations was due to a desire to relieve poor scholars from some of the hardships of their life at the University, by providing buildings in which they could reside, in common, at a moderate cost; and at a very early period "hostels" or "halls" were established by wealthy and benevolent persons for this purpose. It gives a human interest to these ancient walls to think of those who have studied in the rooms which they enclose. Thus, Oriel College, founded in 1326, by Edward II., claims among its students Sir Walter Raleigh, Butler (author of the "Analogy"), Dr. Arnold of Rugby, Archbishop Whately, John Henry Newman, Bishop Wilberforce, and Thomas Hughes. Among those who received their education at "Christ Church" were Sir Thomas More, Sir Philip Sidney, John Locke, Ben Jonson, the Duke of Welling-

BALLIOL COLLEGE, OXFORD.

TRINITY COLLEGE LIBRARY.

ton, Canning, Peel, Ruskin, and Gladstone. "Lincoln" claims among her alumni John Wesley, founder of the Methodists; "Magdalen" has graduated Cardinal Wolsey, Bishop Latimer, John Hampden, Addison the essayist, and Gibbon the historian, as well as the novelists Charles Reade and Wilkie Collins; while "Balliol" has upon its books the names of Adam Smith the economist, Sir William Hamilton the metaphysician, Southey, Swinburne, Lockhart, Dean Stanley, Cardinal Manning, and Matthew Arnold.

In a similar way the various colleges at Cambridge number among their children Jeremy Taylor, Sir Isaac Newton, Edmund Spenser, Milton, Bacon, Dryden, Lord Chesterfield, Wordsworth, Lord Palmerston, Cowley, Herbert, Macaulay, Coleridge, Darwin, Bulwer Lytton, Byron (whose statue by Thorwaldsen adorns the library of Trinity), as well as Thackeray, Tennyson, and John Harvard, the founder of Harvard College in Cambridge, Massachusetts. It is noteworthy, also, that the present Chancellor of Oxford is the Marquis of Salisbury.

THE BODLEIAN LIBRARY, OXFORD.

As might be expected, the libraries of these Universities are of great value, and, in particular, the Bodleian Library at Oxford has but two or three superiors in the world. Founded in 1445, it was formally opened by Sir Thomas Bodley in 1603, who obtained a grant entitling it to a copy of every book copyrighted in England. It now contains about four hundred and sixty thousand printed volumes, twenty-seven thousand volumes of manuscripts, and fifty thousand coins and antiquities. Among the latter are some original drawings by Raphael and Michelangelo; while among its most precious treasures are an edition of Plato brought from Egypt, and, dating from 806 A.D., a manuscript copy of Virgil equally old, and the first Bible printed at Mainz.

Of the two University towns Oxford is the more beautiful. In fact, there is no spot in the whole of England that offers such a perfect combination of Arcadian simplicity of nature and perfection of old Gothic art as Oxford and its environs. Lovers of trees (and who in England can be other than a worshiper of arboriculture?) find here abundant proof that "the groves were man's first temples." Many of Oxford's shady walks, dark with gigantic oaks and elms, suggest cathedral aisles, and near the little river Cherwell, a tributary to the Thames, are solitary promenades, where one may wander, lost in noble reveries, yet held to earth by the most exquisite of natural attractions. He who has strolled, on a fine summer morning, behind old Magdalen College in Addison's walk, when the adjoining trees seemed vibratory with the songs of larks, which had for an accompaniment the murmur of the classic stream, will surely never forget the experience; and it would well repay a visit to Oxford merely to look upon the velvety turf which carpets all its storied courts with an unbroken emerald sward, reaching from finely pebbled paths up to gray walls on which the ivy clings caressingly; for at the sight of these historic halls of culture, embellished by such exquisite surroundings, one thinks of a group of agèd poets, crowned with laurel and seated upon divans buried deep with flowers.

MAGDALEN COLLEGE, OXFORD.

ADDISON'S WALK, OXFORD.

No place that I have ever seen breathes such an atmosphere of mental sweetness and repose; and if one could be a disembodied spirit, and live only in the intellectual, Oxford would be a paradise. It is a beneficial thing for a reflective man of middle life to walk alone, or possibly with some entirely congenial spirit, along the embowered paths of Oxford and Cambridge, or through their quadrangles whose walls have echoed to the footsteps of so many brainy men of England. How many dreams of future greatness have been nurtured here, for one that has been real-

THE LIME WALK, OXFORD.

ized! How many castles have been built upon foundations light as air! How many fond illusions cherished until experience dispelled them as the sun the dew! Yet, even though no great success on the world's stage has been achieved by those whose high ambitions, cradled here, failed subsequently of attainment, the broadened culture they obtained was, probably in most cases, never regretted. For to a thoughtful, refined nature the influence of a classical education, even though it have no practical bearing on the acquisition of money, is of priceless value. It gives a subtile, but recognizable, flavor to the thought and diction of the man who has been trained by it, and through the lense of intellectual sympathy enlarges evermore his mental vision. Like pure, invigorating mountain air, it is a tonic, even though one cannot live by it alone. Whatever happens, it remains a permanent possession and

TRINITY COLLEGE AVENUE, CAMBRIDGE.

QUEEN'S COLLEGE LIBRARY, OXFORD.

an indestructible part of the immortal soul. It is like the depths of the ocean, unruffled by the superficialities that curb and crest its waves; or like the mighty equatorial current that sweeps round the globe, tossing the flotsam and jetsam of the commonplace on shores of which it takes no heed. Realizing its value, the man of middle life feels almost irresistibly impelled to stop the University youths whom he encounters and counsel them to make the most of their rare opportunities, while yet they last; for well he knows that all great mental gains must be the bud and flower of the full, rich spring or early summer of life, not the untimely bloom of autumn. To shape the future, and to be the sculptor of its destiny, is the privilege of youth alone, when

> "Hands of invisible spirits touch the strings
> Of that mysterious instrument, the soul,
> And play the prelude of our fate";

and it is only then that we have courage, after repeated failures, to begin again. Moreover, when the realization of missed or wasted opportunities comes in later years, the loss is usually irreparable; for character has then been formed, the mind is no longer plastic, environment has become rigid, and the iron fetters of circumstances cannot be broken.

> "There are gains for all our losses,
> There are balms for all our pain,
> But when youth, the dream, departs,
> It takes something from our hearts,
> And it never comes again.
>
> We are stronger and are better
> Under manhood's sterner reign;
> Still we feel that something sweet
> Followed youth with flying feet,
> And will never come again.
>
> Something beautiful is vanished,
> And we sigh for it in vain;
> We behold it everywhere,
> On the earth and in the air,
> But it never comes again."

KING'S COLLEGE, CAMBRIDGE.

NEWSTEAD ABBEY.

One hundred and thirty miles from London lies an estate, possessing for all lovers of literature far more interest than Haddon Hall. It is the ancient residence of the Byron family, Newstead Abbey, of which the poet came into possession when about twelve years old. Rarely have I enjoyed an excursion more than that which brought me to this lovely place. It stands in the heart of Sherwood Forest, the ancient haunt of Robin Hood and his famous outlaws; and the approach to it is by a road winding for miles through acres upon acres of old English oaks, some of which have defied the storms of seven hundred years. A few rooms in the fine old mansion, which adjoins the ruined Abbey, remain with their extremely simple furniture and decorations, exactly as when Byron occupied them. So great a difference usually exists between a literary hero's intellectual life, and that which he is wont to lead in the practical details of every-day existence, that a visit to his residence rarely throws any light upon that side of his career and character about which, out of sympathy as well as curiosity, we desire to be informed. But after spending several hours at Newstead Abbey, I felt that I understood the real Lord Byron better than I could have done had I not seen his home and grave. The sight of his little dining-room, for example, naturally recalled one of the most important habits of his life. For Byron suffered from two bodily afflictions,—a deformity in one of his feet, and a tendency to excessive stoutness. But, since his lameness prevented him from checking his increasing corpulence by exercise, he fought against it in a way which made the greater part of his life a torture, and brought him to an early grave. It is well known that to reduce his size, Byron, for several years, almost starved himself, and weakened his constitution by powerful medicines. In one respect this painful regimen repaid him nobly, for it endowed him with a beauty which became proverbial. His features grew clear-cut and delicate, with curves as perfect as if wrought in marble. His lips

SHERWOOD FOREST.

BYRON'S OAK, NEWSTEAD ABBEY.

and chin assumed a peculiar sweetness, that made the lower part of his face seem like that of a bewitching woman rather than a handsome man. Moreover, when he spoke, the fascination of his person was increased; for his voice was exquisitely rich and sweet, and in some houses where he was a guest the children called him "the gentleman who speaks like music." It was a dangerous gift, however, for as he himself tells us:

> "The devil hath not, in all his quiver's choice,
> An arrow for the heart like a sweet voice."

BYRON IN YOUTH.

Of late years the world has been awakened to a juster estimate of Lord Byron. The family traits which he inherited; his sensitive organization; the faults and prejudices of his time; and, above all, the undue violence of public censure, which drove him to defiant scorn, — a recognition of all these has thrown a softer light upon his character. It has been seen that while with most great men their virtues are proclaimed, their faults forgotten, the sins of Byron have been better known than his good qualities; for he was not alone incapable of hiding his own frailties, but frequently was moved, by vanity or caprice, to make himself appear worse than he really was. Moreover, it is now better understood how different his character might have been if he had had a different mother. A worse parent for such a child can hardly be imagined. Although at times indulgent to excess, her temper bordered on insanity. She rarely passed a week without an outburst of hysterical rage. One day, after loading her child with abusive epithets, she mockingly called him "a lame brat." At this outrageous taunt a fearful light came into the child's eyes, but he surpassed his mother in self-control. For a moment his lips quivered and his face whitened; then, very slowly, he spoke these five short words, "I was born so, mother," and turned from the woman who dared not follow him. Yet Byron loved her; and after she was dead, he was found weeping in the dark beside her lifeless form.

THE DINING-HALL, NEWSTEAD ABBEY.

One of the many examples of the poet's eccentricity is the elaborate marble monument, which he caused to be erected in the park of Newstead Abbey, over the grave of a favorite Newfoundland dog, beside which he at one time expressed a desire to be buried.

Apparently Lady Byron did not possess the requisite tact or patience to adapt herself to her husband's peculiar character; and yet such adaptation could not have been very difficult; for, years after, the poet's valet, Fletcher, said, "The only woman I ever saw who could not manage Lord Byron easily was my Lady." On the other hand, it is not right to blame Lady Byron too severely. Experience teaches us that intellectual superiority may command our admiration, but does not, of necessity, win our love. Extraordinary geniuses may fill the world with inspiration, and, nevertheless, be very uncomfortable people to live with day by day. Byron had many causes for unhappiness. He was extremely sensitive, and knew that thousands hated him because he had achieved such wonderful success. Politically, also, he had many enemies. Nine out of every ten Englishmen then thought Washington a traitor to King George, and Bonaparte a fiend incarnate; but Byron openly called Washington the loftiest of heroes, and could not hide his admiration for Napoleon. Thus, after the battle of Waterloo, he wrote: "I feel as if I had taken ipecac — to think that those stupid Bourbons are restored. What right have we to prescribe laws to France? However, the Kings' times are fast vanishing. Those of the people are at hand. I shall not live to see it; but I foresee it. Give me a republic. Look at the history of our earth: Rome, Greece, Venice, Holland,

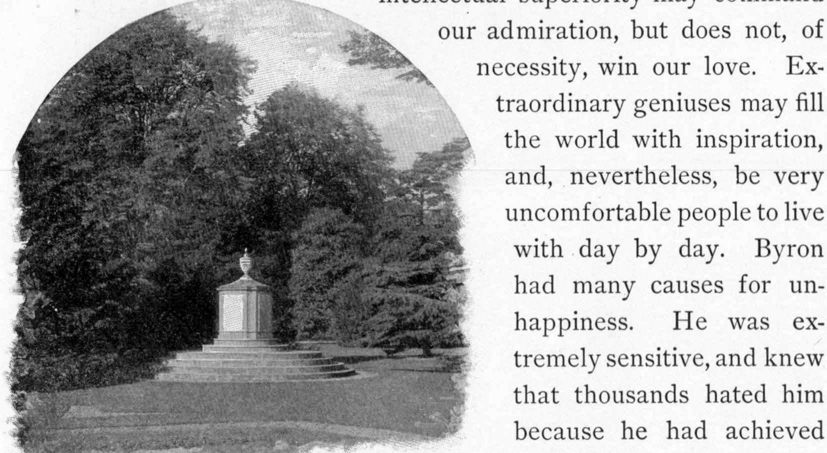

BYRON'S MONUMENT TO HIS DOG.

WICKHAM BRIDGE.

France, America! Compare what they have done as republics to what they did under masters." But this in England then was rank heresy. When, therefore, the scandal of a separation from his wife gave them a pretext, his enemies joined to crush him without mercy. There seemed to Byron to be no alternative. Having lost his home, he must now lose his country; because, as he truly said: "If what is whispered here be true, I am unfit for England; if false, then England is unfit for me."

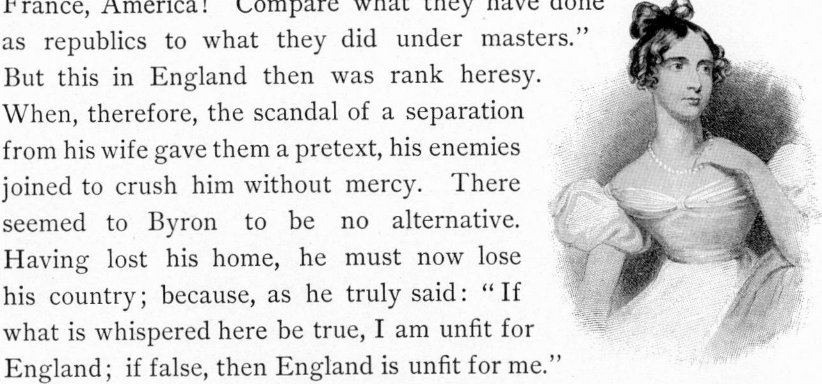

LADY BYRON.

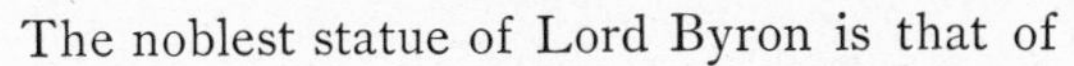

The noblest statue of Lord Byron is that of Thorwaldsen, which represents him seated on a broken column of the Parthenon. It calls to mind the fact that, just as in his youth he had written in Childe Harold the grandest eulogy of Greece that any poet has produced, so when, in 1823, the Greeks endeavored to throw off the Turkish yoke and make themselves a nation, Byron went out at once to aid them, and perished in the attempt. In judging, therefore, of his character, it should never be forgotten that he died at thirty-seven; just at the time when he was on the point of living down the past and building up a nobler future. A Spanish writer has well said: "Many know better how to live than Byron; but few know better how to die." True words; for he was rich, and he renounced his wealth; a poet, and he laid down his pen; beloved, and he forsook the one whom he adored, to die for that most glorious of causes, — human liberty.

THORWALDSEN'S STATUE OF LORD BYRON.

CHURCH WHERE BYRON IS BURIED.

Three miles from Newstead Abbey stands a little church, in which the author of "Childe Harold," after life's fitful fever, now sleeps well. What a contrast between this humble structure and the tomb he might have had at Athens! For the Greeks regarded as one of their own heroes this poet who had sung so grandly of their country, and who had come, all radiant with fame, to lead them on to deeds of glory worthy of their immortal past. They, therefore, wished that his remains should rest on Grecian soil; but English friends insisted on sending his body back to England, supposing, of course, that it would

BYRON'S GRAVE.

AN ENGLISH MILL.

be entombed in Westminster Abbey, or St. Paul's Cathedral. Both these edifices were, however, resolutely closed to its reception. Accordingly on the 12th of July, 1824, Lord Byron was buried beside the body of his mother.

In 1852, Ada, the only child of Lord and Lady Byron, whom he had never seen except in infancy, yet to whom he addressed some of his sweetest lines, was, at her own request (and she was then a woman thirty-five years of age), laid here to rest, not where her mother, Lady Byron, would be buried,— no, but by her father, who had fondly called her "Ada, sole daughter of my house and heart," and on whose lips her name had trembled just before his death. In this connection, it is pathetic to remember that, for years her father's writings and even his portraits had been, as far as possible, kept from that daughter; but she had found and read his poems; and among the lines addressed to her she had discovered these:

ADA.

> "Yet, though dull Hate as duty should be taught,
> I know that thou wilt love me; . . .
> Though the grave closed between us,— 'twere the same:
> I know that thou wilt love me; . . .
> . . . .
> Sweet be thy cradled slumbers! O'er the sea,
> And from the mountains where I now respire,
> Fain would I waft such blessing upon thee,
> As, with a sigh, I dream thou might'st have been to me!"

The prophecy of Byron was fulfilled. The grave had closed between them; but she had loved him with a loyal heart, and in their death father and daughter were united.

Of all English writers the one who has made our old home and its inhabitants best known to us is Charles Dickens. To one familiar with his works Old England is no longer strange. His characters are met at every turn, and landmark after land-

DURHAM CATHEDRAL IN WINTER.

mark in his books is seen and recognized, until we wish that we could go to him and say, as did a simple-hearted citizen of Dublin, "God bless you, Sir, not only for the light of your face, but for the light you've been in my house this many a year"; or act as did a lady of Edinburgh who, her eyes filled with grateful tears, asked him if she might touch the hand which had filled her life with so many friends. Who, for example, can behold an English landscape in the winter time, without a thrill of gratitude to Dickens for all that he has done to make the Christmas season dear to the hearts of old and young throughout the world? Think of his various Christmas stories: "The Chimes," "The Carol," "The Cricket on the Hearth," each one, as it appeared, a Christmas gift of unalloyed pleasure to thousands of expectant readers.

There came to Dickens daily about Christmas time innumerable letters from friends and utter strangers, to tell him how "The Carol," or "The Cricket," had been read around their firesides, and had done no end of good. "Blessings on your kind heart," wrote Jeffrey to him, "you should be happy yourself at Christmas, for by these books you have done more good, fostered more kindly feelings, and prompted more benevolence than can ever be estimated." In truth, Dickens put as much care and energy into his Christmas stories as into his larger works; and over one of them, he says, he wept and laughed and wept again, and walked, while thinking of it, twenty miles through the black streets of London, after all sober folks had gone to bed.

Dickens always held that mental rest is best obtained from bodily exertion. Hence, after some hours of intellectual excitement, he would start out for what he called a "breather," that is, a walk of twenty miles upon the road. Sometimes, when troubled with sleeplessness, he would rise in the dead of night, and walk ten or fifteen miles into the country to breakfast at

"ON AN ENGLISH ROAD."

some tavern. "I half expect," writes one of his friends, "to see him any time, coming along against the wind at the rate of four and a half miles an hour, the very embodiment of energy, and filled to the brim with life."

Some of the happiest hours of my life have been spent in tracing in London and various parts of England the footsteps of Dickens and his characters. When I began to do this, directly after the novelist's death, there was almost no literature on the subject; but now there are several books devoted solely to the identification and preservation of the places mentioned in his novels. London itself, of course, abounds in such localities; but, outside of the city also, one may visit the White Horse Inn at Ipswich, where Mr. Pickwick got into the wrong room; the Kentish marshes, where Pip in "Great Expectations" had his adventure with the escaped convict; Canterbury, with its memories of Agnes, Uriah Heep, and David Copperfield; Brighton, where Little Paul Dombey wondered what the waves were always saying; Yarmouth Beach, where Little Emily lived, and Steerforth was shipwrecked; Barnard's Inn, Yorkshire, where is the school of Squeers, immortalized by Dickens as Do-the-boys Hall; and, above all, Rochester, which figured so prominently in Dickens' works, from one of the

ROCHESTER CATHEDRAL.

ROCHESTER CASTLE.

earliest of them, "The Pickwick Papers," down to the latest and unfinished "Edwin Drood." The last words Dickens ever wrote describe a summer morning in that attractive city, and in its old cathedral there is a tablet reared "to connect his memory with those associations of Rochester Cathedral and its neighborhood which extended over all his life." Dickens was, also, greatly interested in the ancient Castle of Rochester, and, invariably, took his American visitors to see it, relating to them, in his eager and enthusiastic way, its history and legends. In one of the streets of Rochester stands the house of Miss Haversham, the eccentric spinster of "Great Expectations"; and in another thoroughfare the tourist sees the famous Bull Hotel, where the members of the Pickwick Club were lodged on their first excursion from London. In fact, lest there should be any doubt about the identity of this inn, the proprietor has displayed upon a sign, placed near the entrance, the words: "Good House: Nice Beds: *vide* Pickwick." The rest of Dickens' description, however, he is careful not to add; for, as uttered by the loquacious Mr. Jingle, it reads thus: "Stop here? Not I. Dear, very dear. Half a crown in the bill if you look at the waiter. Charge you more if you dine at a

THE BULL HOTEL.

THE "ELEVATED DEN."

friend's than if you dined in the coffee-room. Rum fellows, very." Passing into this hotel, I also saw the room in which the celebrated ball was held; and where the gallery for musicians, called by Dickens "an elevated den," is carefully preserved as a literary landmark of much value.

But far more interesting than any spot described by him, in fiction, is the estate of Gad's Hill where Dickens died. It fronts upon the road that leads from Rochester to London, and was appropriately the last and crowning residence of Dickens' life. For, when a mere child, going up to London, he had looked upon this mansion with such admiration that his father said to him, if he

GAD'S HILL, FROM THE LAWN.

OLD HOUSES IN ROCHESTER.

worked very hard he might possibly some day come to live in such a house. At last, then, his boyish dream was more than realized; and, famous and beloved throughout the world, he came to make this place his home. Here he wrote most of his later works, in easy access to the world of London, which he prized so highly, yet surrounded by meadows, trees, and flowers, which he loved still more; for always, when he wrote, fresh flowers from his garden or conservatory stood upon his desk.

At Christmas and New Year's, Gad's Hill was always full to overflowing, some of his guests having to put up at the village inn. His daughter says that all the intimate friends of Dickens will remember him as he looked on the last midnight of every December, watching the Old Year out and the New Year in. Whatever the weather might be, he would always stand, watch in hand, at the open door listening for the New Year's chimes; and as they rang out on the frosty air, he would exclaim: "A Happy New Year! God bless you all." And then such kissing, hand-shaking, dancing, and drinking of healths in hot mulled wine could never be forgotten by the merry company.

DICKENS AND HIS DAUGHTERS.

Dickens' devotion to his children was remarkable. His daughters speak of it as something extraordinary. His singing to them, for example, before bedtime when they were little children was their greatest delight. He would often do this for

DICKENS' STUDY.

an hour at a time, with one child on each knee and the others standing around him, enjoying it himself as much as any of them. He took the greatest care of the education of his children, and wrote, not only prayers for them to repeat as soon as they were old enough to say them, but also a simple history of the New Testament which they could understand. His "Child's History of England," also, was inspired by the same motive. While, therefore, no man worked more indefat-

THE "MASTER OF HUMOR AND PATHOS."

igably than Charles Dickens, he was never too busy to devote himself to his children's welfare.

An interesting account of how the novelist worked is given by his youngest daughter. One day, when a child, she was recovering from an illness and was allowed to lie on the sofa in his library while he was writing. This she considered a great honor and lay as still as a mouse. For a long time there was no sound but the rapid moving of his pen; when suddenly he jumped up, ran to the mirror, looked at himself in it, distorting his expression in so doing, and then rushed back to his desk. This he repeated several times, talking rapidly to himself all the while and utterly oblivious of his daughter's presence. Undoubtedly he was for the time impersonating one of the characters he was then delineating.

IN THE GROUNDS AT GAD'S HILL.

I shall never forget a visit to the library of Dickens some years after his decease. Sadly I called to mind the last day of his literary labors. It was the early summer. His fingers that morning had turned the calendar on his desk to the 8th of June. The day was beautiful and tempted him to walk that afternoon, as usual, in the woods and fields; but, contrary to his custom, he remained steadily at work. The fatal spectre, whose warnings had been all unheeded, stood within the room, but as yet unperceived. Its shadow fell already on his manuscript, but in the brightness of his fancy he discerned no clouds. Singularly enough, however, these were the words he traced: "Changes of glorious light from moving trees, the songs of birds, the scents from gardens, woods, and fields penetrate the cathedral, subdue its earthy odor, and preach the Resurrection and the Life."

The shadow deepens. He detects its influence. He lays aside his pen; ah! nevermore, O, master of humor and pathos, to be held by thee again. He leaves his study for the last time. The hour of dinner has already come. As he sits down his sister sees upon his face a look of pain. A moment later he rises to his feet, stammers a few words incoherently, then sinks heavily upon his side. The overworked vessels of his gifted brain had burst at last. Slowly and steadily the light which had for years been shining in so many hearts and homes grew fainter and more fitful. At last the watchers heard him give a sigh, saw one tear roll along his beautiful strong face, and he was gone from them.

THE GRAVE OF CHARLES DICKENS.

Then, in his case, were verified the words which he himself

ON THE UPPER THAMES.

had written of little Paul Dombey, when the fair river of his childish life had mingled with the boundless sea: "The golden ripple came again upon the wall, but nothing else stirred in the room. The old, old fashion, Death. O! thank God, all who see it, for the older fashion yet of immortality, and look upon us, angels of young children, with regards not quite estranged when the swift river bears us to the ocean."

It is in that unrivaled shrine of English genius, Westminster Abbey, that Dickens lies buried. He would have preferred to lie in the small graveyard under Rochester Castle, or in some favorite cemetery that he knew and loved; but the English press, the nobility, and the nation at large united in respectfully requesting that this last honor should be paid him by his country. Accordingly privately and with no ostentation, as he had especially directed in his will, on the 14th of June, 1870, all that was mortal of the great novelist was, by his relatives and dearest friends, laid here to rest. But later in the day, and all the following day, the aisles were thronged with countless mourners, and on his grave flowers were strewn by many unknown hands, and tears were shed by many unknown eyes. So it is even to the present time. No need, O Dickens! to enumerate the causes of our grief beside thy grave. Some characters of thy creation are dear to us as lifelong friends. Greater than in the chapels of dead kings are here the reverence

CHARLES DICKENS.

and love we feel for thee; for thou, by thine own genius, didst create an empire whose subjects are continually increasing and can never die. No, when the Abbey itself shall have fallen into ruin, when even thy tomb may be unknown, thy works will live, and thousands as they read will still be moved to laughter or to tears and bless thy memory as I, a grateful pilgrim, did with faltering lips when standing on thy grave.

LONDON

MARLBOROUGH HOUSE.

THE sailor on our inland seas — Superior, Michigan, and Huron — is probably as brave and hardy as the ocean mariner. He has met tempests quite as fierce as any known to the Atlantic, and his instinctive courage has been forged to a finer temper by knowing that the narrow limits of the lakes continually threaten him with what the deep-sea sailor dreads even more than fog, — a treacherous lee shore. But if, in a moment of unconsciousness, he could be suddenly lifted with his ship and launched upon the ocean, he would on waking, even though in darkness, feel that some startling change had taken place in his surroundings. He would perceive it in the saline breeze and the long roll of the Atlantic, and would divine that, somehow, there had come between him and the solid bed-rock of the globe a greater depth, as well as a wider offing between ship and

REGENT STREET.

FLEET STREET AND ST. PAUL'S.

shore. So, when a stranger enters London, even though he has been accustomed to life in a large city, he recognizes at once that here is something superior to anything he has ever known. He feels the life-surge of humanity uplifting him, as the transported mariner of the lakes perceives beneath his ship the undulating swell that has swept half way round the world. The rattle of wheels, the beat of horses' feet, and the great city's ceaseless roar are in detail not unlike what he has heard elsewhere; yet underneath it all, he feels there is a difference, and as he makes his way amid the throng along the Strand, watches the endless tide of human life ebbing and flowing across London Bridge, drifts down the crowded Thames, from Hammersmith to Greenwich, or hears the ponderous peal of "Great Paul" in the tower of St. Paul's, half smothered by the tumult of the streets, he realizes with a sentiment akin to awe that he is standing in the world's metropolis.

In truth, of all great cities, London is the greatest. It is the most powerful magnet of mental, moral, and material forces man has ever made. Hither are drawn the most ambitious, active, and ingenious of Old England's offspring; and here are formed the literary, naval, military, and commercial plans that make of London a colossal concentration of vitality, the influences of which extend around the globe. Even its antiquity is impressive; for London is more than two thousand years old. It was a British settlement when Julius Cæsar landed near the Dover cliffs; it, subsequently, heard the trumpets of the Roman legions, and the Emperor Claudius tried to rob it of its name; yet, only seven hundred years ago, although already thirteen centuries old, it contained less than fifty thousand inhabitants; and five more centuries of growth were needed to raise its population to two hundred thousand. It had not reached a million, even, at the opening of this century; but now, in the amazing hive of human

TOTTENHAM COURT ROAD.

existence, included within the Metropolitan Police District of London, more than five and a half million men, women, and children feast or starve, achieve or fail, amuse themselves or suffer, till, having played their several parts upon this murky stage, they are replaced by others. There are more people here than in all the New England States combined, or than in the whole of Switzerland, and more than twice as many as in Norway.

London contains more Irishmen than Dublin, more Scotchmen than Edinburgh, and more Jews than all Palestine. Every four minutes a human soul is added to its population, and at a little longer interval one disappears. London has been described as a province covered with houses; and, in fact, its buildings, looked on from the cupola of St. Paul's, appear to be a limitless expanse of swarming ant-hills, separated by innumerable sluices, through which at every hour of the day and night the stream of life, now clear and pure, now thick and slimy, pours on, or curdles on, God alone knows whither. In evading pursuit,

WHITEHALL.

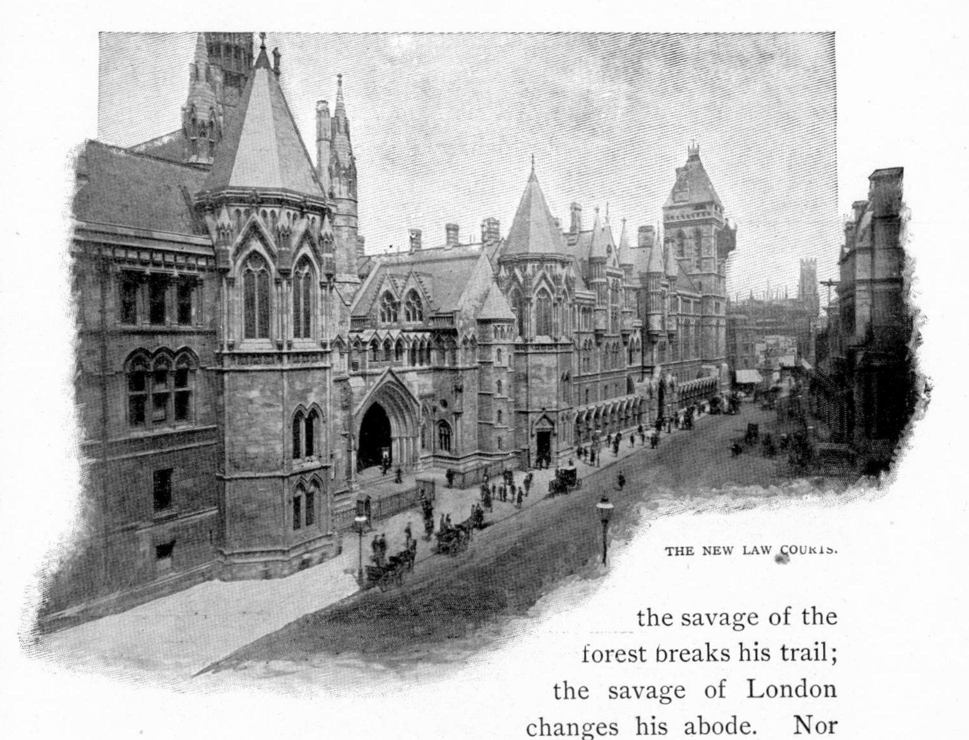

THE NEW LAW COURTS.

the savage of the forest breaks his trail; the savage of London changes his abode. Nor is the latter feat especially difficult; for this metropolitan world has about seven thousand miles of streets, to go through all of which would be equivalent to walking across the American continent and back. Moreover, London is still growing! Every year about seventy miles of new streets are added to the bewildering network of its thoroughfares, and, on the average, every twenty minutes a new building is joined to its gigantic frame. It is not strange, therefore, that such a city's stock of names should soon become exhausted. There are said to be at present within the limits of London ninety-five King Streets, ninety-nine Queen Streets, seventy-eight Prince Streets, one hundred and twenty-seven York Streets, and eighty-seven James Streets, so that some other distinguishing title has in each case to be affixed.

Samuel Johnson once declared, "The full tide of existence is at Charing Cross," and the statement seems justified when we enter the railway station of that name, where thousands come and go on lines of steel which, while communicating with the remotest sections of the earth, seem to converge and centre here, as formerly "all roads led to Rome." A part of this leviathan of stone is the Charing Cross Hotel, which serves as a colossal net to catch the human fish that swarm up hither from the sea, and hold them until they can be properly distributed. It is a cosmopolitan caravansary; in which, as in a Russian prison, a number rather than a name is given to each inmate, who, therefore, timidly requests from one of the maids in the office "Number 47's bill," or falteringly deprecates an overcharge for "the light of other days" with a dread of encountering a supercilious "Ah! — Indeed? — Really!" kind of stare. In the Charing Cross Hotel the homesick tourist feels like a prisoner in the Tower of Babel; for he hears all languages spoken about him except English, jostles Turks upon the staircase, and rides with Chinamen in the sepulchral "lift." Even the waiters in this hostelry are foreigners, many of whom are studying so earnestly the language of the Britons that they have no time to attend to the guests. This busy centre of London is hardly the place where one would look for any evidence of sentiment, yet

CHARING CROSS HOTEL.

LONDON BRIDGE.

directly in front of the enormous railway station and hotel of Charing Cross, springs, like a graceful flower, from the pavement, a beautiful Gothic spire in honor of the wife of Edward I., the beautiful Queen Eleanor, whose name has been associated with this spot more than six hundred years. It was this "Queen of good memory" who, despite all remonstrances, accompanied her husband through the dangers and privations of the seventh and last Crusade, saying, "Nothing ought to part those whom God hath joined, and the way to heaven is as near from Palestine as from England." On the route of her funeral procession from Lincoln to Westminster Abbey, where her loved form was finally laid to rest, nine halting-places were chosen, at each of which for a time the body of the Queen reposed. At each of these stations a cross was erected, the last and most elaborate being here. Hence many have supposed that the present name of the locality is derived from the hasty, anglicized pronunciation of "*Chère Reine*" Cross; but the inexorable philologists now tell us that the more probable derivation of the name is the Saxon word Charan, meaning "to turn." The original cruciform memorial to the "dear Queen" was destroyed by the Puritans, in 1647; but, happily, the tender thought that built and for four hundred years preserved it has not perished, and is suggested by the present

THE ELEANOR CROSS.

Gothic spire. I have called it beautiful, and so it would be could it be restored to its original whiteness; but the inevitable soot of London has discolored it, so that its sculptured elegance is largely lost, and its appearance is almost that of a bronze shaft flecked with snow.

From the court of Charing Cross Hotel one steps directly into the flood of life that rushes through that most

A PORTION OF THE STRAND.

renowned of London thoroughfares, — the Strand. That this was once, as its name indicates, the shore of the Thames now seems incredible; but such is the fact, and as late as 1315 a petition was presented to the King complaining that the road was infamously bad, and overgrown with thickets and bushes. Later, the Strand became for three hundred years the favorite abode of the English aristocracy, whose gardens sloped from their palatial residences to the river bank, and caused this portion of the Thames to be compared to the Grand Canal of

Venice. To-day, however, those stately palaces have disappeared, and the Strand and its continuation, Fleet Street, are now so thoroughly devoted to business interests that a "Hair Cutting Saloon," as its sign conspicuously states, has replaced a residence of Henry VIII. and Cardinal Wolsey.

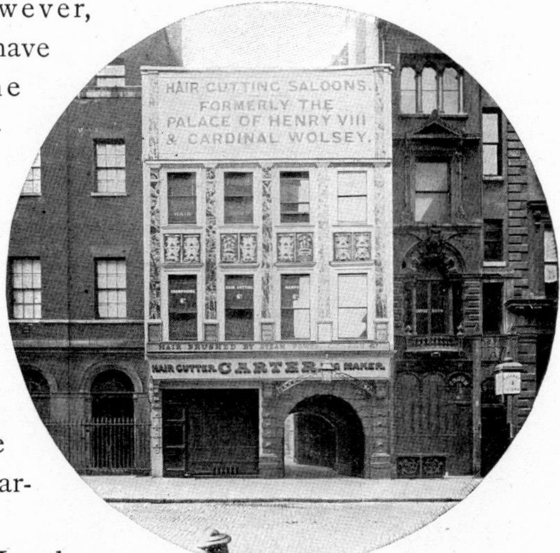

PALACE AND BARBER SHOP.

On my first visit to London, one of its most interesting objects was a grimy gateway, known as Temple Bar, which had for centuries marked the terminus of the Strand and the commencement of the "City" proper. The contracted opening of this gate, at the converging point of two congested thoroughfares, reminded me of an hour-glass through which the sands of life were running fast; and I could understand the sentiment of Doctor Johnson, when he said: "It is my practice, when I am in want of amuse-

OLD TEMPLE BAR.

ment, to place myself for an hour at Temple Bar, and examine, one by one, the looks of the passengers."

It seems a pity to have destroyed this celebrated landmark of Old London, as was done in 1878. Without too much impediment to traffic, another arch could certainly have been constructed here, which by a preservation of the ancient form, at least, would have reminded one of its historic predecessor; but now the memory of Temple Bar is guarded only by an unimpressive column, surmounted by a dragon, and adorned with statues of the Queen and the Prince of Wales. The sentiment of which that ancient portal was the symbol was peculiar; since it defined the respective powers of the English Sovereign and the Lord Mayor of London, who, by the way, is not the Mayor of the whole metropolis, but only of the "City." The latter was tenacious of his rights, and whenever the King or Queen of England desired to enter his domain, Temple Bar was always closed until, after an interchange of courtesies, the gateway was thrown open, and the Lord Mayor presented the keys of the city to his royal master who at once returned them. Such was the ceremony enacted here when Elizabeth went to

THE TEMPLE BAR MEMORIAL.

BUCKINGHAM PALACE.

St. Paul's Cathedral to thank God for the destruction of the Spanish Armada; and again, in 1649, when Cromwell passed within the "City" to dine in state, and so it has been with Queen Victoria, whenever she has made her public entries into oldest London. Here, also, in the days when a display of ghastly horrors was thought to keep men from committing crimes, the heads or limbs of those who had been executed for

THE STRAND, LOOKING WEST.

high treason were exhibited. Occasionally, too, the living suffered here. It was, for example, in front of Temple Bar that the impostor, Titus Oates, held up to the derision of the public, was pelted with rotten eggs and dead cats; and here, on the contrary, Defoe — the author of "Robinson Crusoe" — also placed in the pillory for criticism of the Government, enjoyed a perfect ovation from the people, who drank his health and wreathed the arch with flowers. The environs of Temple Bar are rich in literary memories. In fact, for one who takes delight in English literature and its heroes, London has a fascination incomparably greater than that of any other city in the world. For, in every period of English history, the strong thinkers, able writers, and inspired poets of the kingdom have naturally gravitated hither, and from this centre of mentality the influence of their thought has radiated over the entire earth. Associations with great names in letters bloom like flowers along the historic pathway of Old England; and there is scarcely one of the older parts of London that is not made attractive by some literary charm, from the site of the Old Tabard Inn, whence Chaucer's Canterbury Pilgrims set out in the early dawn of English poetry, down to the places linked imperishably with the wit and pathos of Charles Dickens. In Cheapside, for example, is the site of the Mermaid Tavern, where Shakespeare, Ben Jonson, Beaumont, Fletcher, and other members of the brilliant circle of their day, were wont to meet; and in the same locality, a few generations later, was born the poet who made "Paradise" the subject of his song. On the Adelphi Terrace is the

LINCOLN'S INN.

GOLDSMITH'S GRAVE.

house (now let in "chambers") where David Garrick lived and died; and, not a stone's throw from the Strand, within the shadow of the Temple Church, is the grave of Goldsmith.

In King Street, Westminster, we tread a Via Dolorosa where Edmund Spenser, the poet laureate of chivalry and fairy-land, died of starvation and a broken heart. In Bow Street, Covent Garden, stands the house in which the novelist Fielding wrote "Tom Jones"; and we may still behold, near the memorial of Temple Bar, the site of

THE SHAKESPEARE FOUNTAIN.

FLEET STREET.

the Mitre Tavern where Shakespeare and his friends, and, later, Samuel Johnson, Boswell, Goldsmith, and their boon companions fought those duels, whose bullets were light *bon mots*, and whose rapier cuts were thrusts of repartee. Fleet Street has been for centuries a thoroughfare of literature and is, to-day, the heart of London journalism, containing the publishing offices of many periodicals, and of such newspapers as *The Daily Telegraph*, *The Standard*, *The News*, *The Chronicle*, and *Punch;* while in the purlieus of that avenue of printing-power are countless reminiscences of England's most illustrious authors, essayists, and poets. Thus, at No. 17, Gough Square, just off Fleet Street, Samuel

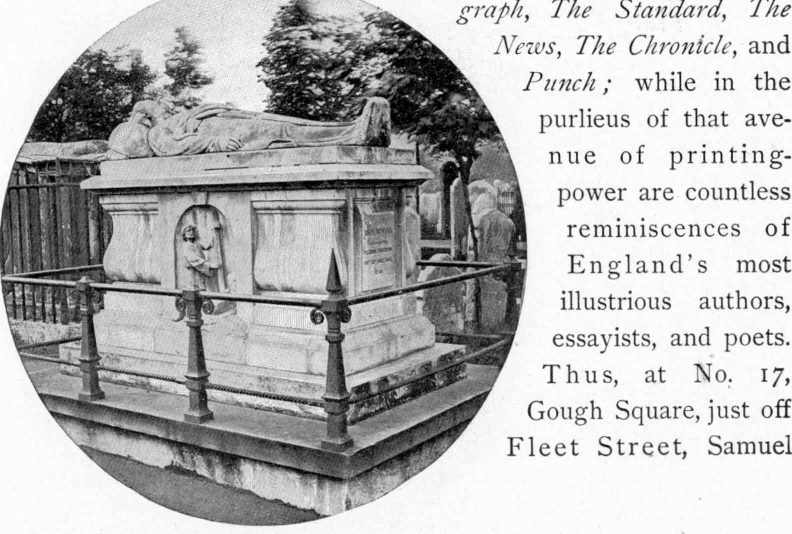

BUNYAN'S TOMB

Johnson completed his famous Dictionary, and, at No. 8, Bolt Court, close by the highway that he loved so well, he spent the last years of his life, and died in 1784. Where the printing-office of *Punch* now stands John Milton once taught school, and in the Cheshire Cheese Tavern one may ensconce himself by the same window, and in the same corner, where the authors of "Rasselas" and the "Vicar of Wakefield" used to sit together. In Fleet Street, Isaac Newton attended the meetings of the Royal Society, of which he was president; and, at the corner of that street and Chancery Lane, two hundred and sixty years ago, stood the milliner's shop of Izaak Walton, the author of the "Complete Angler" and the patron saint of fishermen; while, it was "in a dark letter box, in a dark office, up a dark court in Fleet Street," that Dickens, as he tells us in the preface to his "Pickwick Papers," dropped his first contribution to the press, and started on the road to literary immortality.

A LONDON CROWD.

In driving from Charing Cross down into the heart of Old London, the tourist should on one occasion at least take a hansom, if only to admire the marvelous skill of London cab drivers in winding through the throngs of vehicles and pedestrians

MANSION HOUSE STREET.

which surge through the "City's" narrow streets. It is, probably, the peculiar position from which a hansom cabby looks upon the hubs of his own and his neighbors' wheels that enables him to estimate to almost a hair's breadth the space required for him to pass; but nothing I have ever seen in any other portion of the world can equal the ability thus displayed. The regulation of the traffic in London streets seems as smooth as their pavements. London policemen reign supreme, and their authority is instantly recognized on the mere lifting of the hand. Owing to this and to the absence of tracks and trolley cars, tangles and blocks of vehicles are much less frequent in London

IN THE "CITY."

than in New York; and if a horse falls on the slippery wood or asphalt, a man is always ready to dart forth with a shovel full of sand or gravel (purposely stored at regular intervals along the streets), and scatter it under the animal, so as to aid it in its struggles to regain its foothold. Noticeable, too, are the little spaces, surrounded by pillars, which rise in the centre of these thoroughfares, like islands in a roaring torrent. Indeed, it would be dangerous, and almost impossible, to cross many of London's streets but for these places of refuge, in which pedestrians may halt, while the vehicles roll by on either side.

A LONDON OMNIBUS.

Those who are nervous when driving in a cab through crowds, should mount the London omnibuses, which always carry fully as many passengers without as within; for there, serene in their security from mishaps, they can watch complacently their ponderous battleship plow its way among the lighter craft of London's troubled waters. In fact, long omnibus drives in London (and they can be taken for great distances) are to be strongly recommended, as giving one a better idea of certain portions of the city than can be obtained by any other mode of conveyance. Nor is the acquaintance of a London omnibus driver to be despised; for never will you thoroughly appreciate Sam Weller and his father until you chat with the driver of a London coach. These Jehus, as a rule, are of enormous size, with cheeks so red and oleaginous that, at the slightest puncture with a needle, one might expect a stream of ale or bitter beer to flow; yet they are usually loquacious (when induced to be) and if you slip a shilling into their hands and ask them to point out the notable sights, you will soon roar with laughter, and have a fund of amusement to look back on for a month to come.

OMNIBUS RIDING.

A far more rapid mode of transportation here is London's underground railway, but few metropolitan means of conveyance are so disagreeable. The smell of smoke, the oily, humid atmosphere of coal gas, the single jet of fog-dimmed light in the roof of the railway carriage, which causes the half-illumined passengers to look like wax figures in a "Chamber of Horrors," and, finally, the intricate system of changes necessary at junctions, which one must sometimes make with the agility of an acrobat, do not impart a very cheerful tone to recollections of such subterranean transit. Still, as a colossal scheme of engineering, it commands admiration; and the herculean task can be appreciated only by estimating what it meant to cut these winding thorough-

ST. JAMES' PALACE.

AN UNDERGROUND STATION.

fares through endless labyrinths of pipes and sewers, and under the foundations of enormous buildings. Thus, when we remember the care that must be exercised in giving to sewer pipes a proper inclination toward their termini, we can faintly imagine the difficulties involved in carrying the tunnels for this double-tracked railway *five times* across one conduit which conveys the sewage of fifty thousand houses from Highgate to the Thames. Some of the buildings, too, beneath which trains now run, on an average, every three minutes during the twenty-four hours, were built on piles; a fact which, as the edifices had to be left intact, necessitated not only excellent engineering skill, but, also, a great expenditure of money. Thus, on each of its first twenty-two miles the Metropolitan Underground Railway Company spent two and a half million dollars!

No part of the world that I have ever seen can equal London's underground stations in their display of advertisements.

From the black throat of one tunnel to the cavernous maw of another, the intervening walls are lined with placards of all shapes and sizes and every color of the rainbow; some representing hair "restored," in undulating waves which look like dusky waterfalls; others portraying "works of art," which call attention to the wonderful advantages of plasters, soaps, or spectacles; while all of them furnish loiterers abundant reading facilities, by means of letters visible at a hundred yards to even the most myopic traveler. That this display lights up the Rembrandt shadows of the subterranean stations cheerfully, must be admitted. Its only drawback is the fact that the bewildering variety sometimes causes inexperienced travelers to hunt for the station's name as frantically as passengers in American drawing-room cars look for the chair numbers; which, as we all well know, are usually hidden with an ingenuity that has spoiled many a naturally gentle disposition, and caused the impatient tourist to recall the Arab proverb, "The word that escapes you is your master."

LONDON BRIDGE.

Of all the bridges that cross the Thames, none is so famous as that which bears the appropriate name of London. Moreover, until the recent construction of the new Tower Bridge,

ALBERT MEMORIAL HALL.

it had the distinction of being the last to span the volume of the Thames, and was the nearest to the sea, which is about sixty miles away. Opened to traffic in 1831, its cost was about eight millions of dollars, and the lamp-posts along its sides are said to have been cast from cannon captured from the French in Spain. It is not, however, the external features of this granite viaduct that make it fascinating to the student of humanity and history. It is the fact that this great artery of London's mighty frame, more than aught else, suggests the vastness of the city. A soldier in a battle knows little of what is going on beyond the narrow limits of his own position. He cannot tell whether, across the ridge, or in the shadow of the forest, his friends are being beaten, or are vanquishing the foe; but he does know that he is participating in a general engagement of great magnitude; and, in the breathless pauses of the conflict just around him, he hears the muffled throb of distant guns, the multitudinous rattle of musketry, the bugle's piercing notes, the roll of drums and shouts of maddened men, all of which form together the colossal roar of battle. So he who stands on London Bridge perceives, instinctively, a vast pervading undertone of deep-voiced life beyond the immediate torrent of humanity which is rolling on as con-

WESTMINSTER BRIDGE.

THE INNER TEMPLE.

stantly, and in as undiminished volume, as the Thames beneath.

In view of the immensity of London and its constant traffic, it may appear to some incredible that the French novelist, Daudet, was sincere when he declared that what impressed him most in Britain's capital was its stillness; yet every observant tourist knows that the remark was not a paradox. London is the most silent of great cities, not only from its admirable and comparatively noiseless pavements of wood or asphalt, but from its numerous enclosures, courts, and "inns," from which the roar of the metropolis is so entirely excluded that the effect is delightful. Dickens described this perfectly when he said of Staple Inn: "It is one of these nooks, the turning into which out of the clashing street imparts to the relieved pedestrian the sensation of having put cotton in his ears and velvet soles on his boots." Some of these islands in a sea of

THE MIDDLE TEMPLE.

sound are picturesque, quaint areas, where lawyers have had chambers and literary men studios for more than a hundred years; while others, like the enormous buildings of the Temple and Lincoln's Inn, are both imposing in appearance and rich in historic memories. These are, indeed, ideal places for the student, since they combine retirement and quiet, with close proximity to the life of the city. "High thinking" is not necessarily born in solitude. To the disciplined thinker a secluded life is neither necessary nor beneficial. The forces that sustain and stimulate the race, to-day, are born of friction and association, and are developed, not in the country, but in cities; and even if the modern man does seek retirement to recuperate his strength, he will employ that strength in contact with his fellows.

Far down the river, at the eastern extremity of the "Old City," stands the famous Tower of London. The name is misleading; for, judging merely from its title, the visitor would expect to find one solitary tower rising above the Thames, as Hadrian's Mausoleum frowns upon the Tiber. In reality, however, the Tower of London contains many towers, being a vast expanse of venerable strongholds, turrets, walls, and

THE TOWER, FROM THE RIVER.

bastions encompassed on three sides by a deep moat, and guarded on the fourth by "Father Thames." Still, as there is a "City" within London itself, so in the area of twenty-six acres occupied by the Tower, there is one structure in particular which

THE WHITE TOWER.

antedates all its associates. This bears the name of the White Tower, not, certainly, because its history is spotless, but from the fact that formerly its walls were painted white. It is the oldest palace-prison (not a ruin) in the world; and yet, undoubtedly, a Roman fortress preceded it, and the White Tower rests upon foundations laid by legionaries from the Tiber. It was William the Conqueror, who, in 1078, caused this old Norman fortress to be built, and a more durable edifice would be hard to find. One hundred feet high, one hundred feet square, its grim and haggard features have defied the tempests of eight hundred years.

THE BELL TOWER.

It is as strong to-day as when its Norman architect pronounced it finished; and we may well believe that it will last indefinitely, since its exterior is from twelve to fifteen feet thick, and its apartments are divided from one another by walls ten feet in thickness, which rise from the foundation to the roof. The subsequent accretions to this sombre pile, known by such names as the Middle Tower, Bloody Tower, Beauchamp Tower, and Bell Tower, all served a purpose once, when this enclosure was for about six hundred years the fortified abode of English royalty. The world contains no sadder memorial of man's inhumanity to man than London Tower. For centuries it was the home of sorrow and despair. The record of the victims of despotic cruelty who have endured imprisonment and suffered death within its walls renders one sick at heart, until he realizes that increasing civilization has at last made such atrocities impossible.

THE BLOODY TOWER.

What memories cluster about the old White Tower, which stands with its attendant structures like a dark-browed king surrounded by his vassals! Hence many an English sovereign has gone forth to his coronation, and from its gloomy vault the gallant Wallace was led out to meet a death which was preceded by atrocious torture. Here fratricidal crimes, recalling the barbaric Orient, have been committed, as when the Duke of Clarence, brother of Edward IV., was put to death; or when the young king, Edward V., and his brother Richard — the Princes of the Tower — were cruelly murdered. In 1244, the Prince of Wales, while attempting to escape by a rope made out of his bedclothes, fell to a frightful death in the deep moat. In many instances the only fault of those who were imprisoned here, or put to death, was that they were of royal blood, and, therefore, possible claimants of the throne. Others were victims of court intrigues, royal jealousy, or kingly lust, such as the wives of Henry VIII., Katherine Howard, a queen of eighteen months, and Anne Boleyn, praying with her last breath for her brutal husband, who on the next day married Jane Seymour. Here was beheaded, after a captivity of eighteen years, the gallant, handsome, intellectual explorer and historian, Sir Walter Raleigh, of whom Prince Henry said, "No man but my father would keep such a bird in such a cage." Bishops and priests have met their doom on Tower Hill for having refused to recognize a sovereign's supremacy. Jews, also, have been tortured in these dungeon vaults until they gave up the last penny of their property. Even Love has numbered here his victims, such as the Duke of Norfolk, who had aspired to the hand of Mary, Queen of Scots; while in a room, still shown to the visitor, died the last lord of Wilton, after eleven years of imprisonment, accused of having wished to

THE TOWER CUSTODIANS (THE BEEF-EATERS).

THE TOWER AND TOWER BRIDGE.

TRAITOR'S TOWER.

marry, without the permission of James I., Lady Arabella Stuart, who herself died in the Tower, hopelessly insane. Here, also, some high-spirited men like Henry Percy, Earl of Northumberland, have committed suicide; and here an unfortunate illegitimate son of Henry VIII., imprisoned to avoid embarrassing complications, died of a broken heart; while as a soldiers' monument often covers the remains of countless unknown heroes, so we may be assured that those recorded on the page of history are but a handful to the unnamed, unremembered victims who suffered agony here without a trial, and passed through death into oblivion, as an abandoned swimmer sinks into the sea.

SIR WALTER RALEIGH'S CELL.

THE TRAITOR'S GATE.

One of the most interesting features of the Tower is the Traitor's Gate, the former entrance from the river. The Thames once laved the steps which still lead to a gloomy structure called the Bloody Tower, and we may yet discern the ring to which were moored the boats that brought here their hapless freight. The walls beside this gate are pierced with loopholes through which the wardens of the Tower, as they watched unseen the coming prisoner, could determine, before he landed, whether he had been condemned to death; since, if a fatal sentence had been passed, the Ax of Office,

THE ARCHWAY OF THE BLOODY TOWER.

carried by the escort, always had its sharp edge turned significantly toward the captive. It was at the summit of these steps, as Sir Thomas More was being led to his dungeon, that his daughter, Margaret, seeing the fatal sign of the reversed ax, burst through the crowd, and, flinging herself upon his neck, besought his blessing with such piteous cries that even the guards were moved to tears, while Sir Thomas, as she was torn from his clasp, implored her to resign herself to God's will, and to bear her loss with patience.

Beneath this frowning gateway, also, gentle Anne Boleyn, wearing the dress in which she had been hurried hither from a tournament, without a hint of the nature of her accusation or warning of her dreadful fate, fell on her knees and prayed God to defend her innocence. Eighteen years later her daughter Elizabeth cried, as she passed beneath this arch, "Here landeth as true a subject, being a prisoner, as ever landed on these stairs"; and when she subsequently reëntered the Tower as sovereign, she too knelt down and thanked Almighty God "for an escape as miraculous as that of Daniel out of the mouths of the lions." To stand at night, alone, beside the Traitor's Gate, and think upon the long, long line of the condemned who have passed beneath its scowling masonry, would make excusable a superstitious dread of seeing their restless

THE SITE OF THE SCAFFOLD.

ghosts move by in a procession, ghastly with headless forms, and horrible with clanking chains. Not long ago, a few days after paying a visit to the Tower, I attended a meeting of workingmen in London, where socialists were openly denouncing the British Government, and hundreds were singing, "Down with the Queen and the Throne!" A few policemen were on hand to keep the people within bounds; but no attempt was made to silence them. Contrast that freedom of speech with the cruelty, torture, and death which would have followed such remarks three centuries ago. Truly, in spite of many checks, the world grows gradually wiser, safer, and better.

QUEEN ELIZABETH'S ARMORY.

> "Not long shall evil's gloomy night
> In darkness hold our captive souls;
> Forever into broadening light
> The earth with sun-born impulse rolls."

Since the time of Elizabeth, the Tower has not been a residence of royalty, and is now principally used as a gigantic armory. Its stock of weapons is said to be sufficient to equip a quarter of a million soldiers, and in the ancient banquet-hall alone are arms enough for one hundred and fifty thousand men. Here, too, are kept innumerable trophies won by British valor in all quarters of the globe; and in the Treasure Room are pre-

THE HORSE ARMORY.

served the glorious crown jewels and insignia of the kingdom. Protected by an iron screen, and carefully guarded by armed attendants, the coronation orb, the sceptre, crown, swords, spurs, necklaces, and baptismal fonts of royalty, together with the magnificent gold plate for coronation banquets, lie glittering in a brilliant light, and are valued at fifteen millions of dollars. At this point the voices of the guides, who are still known by their old name of "Beef-eaters," always sound a triumphant pæan; and in response the average subject of Victoria falls down before the royal emblems, as did the subjects of Nebuchadnezzar at the sound of sackbut, psaltery, and harp; while "Oh"s, "Ah"s, and "Just fancy"s resound on every side. For my

THE CROWN JEWELS.

THE WARDEN ON NIGHT WATCH.

part, however, I was soon ready to withdraw from the jostling crowd, and step back into a corner of the room, where a friend narrated to me how, in the reign of Charles II., an Irishman named Thomas Blood very nearly succeeded in carrying off this treasure. Through a pretended illness on the part of his wife, who was kindly taken to the keeper's rooms, Blood formed an acquaintance with the guardian of the jewels, and, finally, proposed a marriage between his son and the keeper's daughter. Later, returning with the alleged bridegroom and two friends, Blood was taken with them, as guests of the family, to see the jewels; whereupon he and his accomplices beat the custodian senseless, and

ORNAMENTAL TROPHIES.

SEVEN DIALS, ST. GILES.

seized the regalia. Fortunately an alarm was given, and the thieves, though they had actually reached the street with the crown and sceptre, were arrested, and the treasure was recovered; yet, strange to say, Blood so contrived to terrify King Charles, by warning him of the vengeance which his friends would take in case of his execution, that he was not only released, but was allowed a pension of twenty-five hundred dollars a year; while the poor old keeper, who had been nearly beaten to death by the ruffians, was allowed to die in poverty.

Into the "East End" of London, beyond the Tower, few tourists care to go, unless on errands of philanthropy or in the study of sociology. The recollection of a few hours passed there in the company of an officer has left an ineffaceable impression of sadness on my memory. That the extent and hopelessness of the misery prevailing there are appalling is evidenced by Englishmen themselves. Certainly, nothing worse could be said of the slums of London than is found in the pathetic pages of Charles Dickens; and, still more recently, they have been described by an English archbishop as "Hell without the fire." Professor Huxley, also, President of the Royal Society, has said of this part of London: "I have several times traveled around the globe, visiting, as I journeyed, the most savage and degraded peoples in barbarous lands; but

NEWGATE PRISON.

I have never anywhere seen such degradation and misery as I have seen in the east end of my own city." Who can wonder, then, that many, weary of such an existence, fling their poor, half-starved, suffering bodies into the Thames,

> "Mad from life's history,
> Glad to death's mystery,
> Swift to be hurled,
> Anywhere, anywhere,
> Out of the world"?

Yet London is not heartless. Its charity is only less colossal than its poverty; for it gives away, in proportion to its population, more than twice as much as is given by any other city in England, and four times the amount bestowed in charity by any city on the Continent.

AMONG THE POOR.

To one who stands beside the Thames, comparisons present themselves between the imperial cities, respectively the capitals, of the past and present, — Rome and London. It is, for example, a remarkable fact that the two mightiest empires of the world have had their capitals situated on comparatively unimportant streams, and that the cities located on these diminutive rivers have become, in turn, the central ganglia from which the vital nerve forces of the Roman and the British governments have successively radiated through the world. There are, however, noticeable differences in these waterways. Their appearance, for example, is entirely dissimilar; for, unlike the tawny Tiber, colored by the clays through which it flows, the Thames rolls onward to its fate almost as free from sedimentary impurities as is the sea that welcomes it. Again, the difference in the amount of their commerce is enormous. The Tiber, even where it gilded with its yellow waves the sandals of Imperial Rome, was barely three hundred feet in width, and at its entry into the Mediterranean, sixteen miles away, had scarcely doubled these dimensions. Hence, few ships gathered at the port of Rome, partly because of the Tiber's contracted size, and partly, also, because the commerce of those days was insignificant compared with that of the present time. To the

THE THAMES, AND TOWER OF LONDON.

THE VICTORIA EMBANKMENT.

ancients, the navigable world was virtually limited to the Mediterranean, which was, indeed, a Roman lake; but to the modern Briton the Thames is but a doorway to a liquid plain whereon he circumnavigates the globe; and the Atlantic, from a boundary, has become a highway, much as the air which, to the fledgeling in the nest appears a barrier, becomes the element through which the free bird cleaves its fearless way from clime to clime.

Is it not possible to trace a similarity between these streams and the two empires whose capitals have adorned their banks? The Tiber, at its terminus, is the same narrow, turbid current it has always been, and, like that river, Rome herself was narrow in her contact with the world. She conquered, but it was for Rome alone, and to her seven hills she brought back captives, to fight as gladiators in her amphitheatres, or toil as slaves for her patricians; while the best works of art and other treasures of the conquered swelled the triumphal pageants of the Sacred

Way. She taught humanity the reign of law, but it was always Roman law, interpreted in favor of the Romans. Wherever the imperial eagles flew, Rome branded on her provinces the seal of her indomitable will; but strove so little to promote their individual welfare that, finally, she fell, because the conqueror and the conquered were but artificially united. The English river, on the contrary, although at London only nine hundred feet from bank to bank, rolls onward in an ever-widening channel, until it greets the ocean in an estuary six miles broad. Similarly, the Anglo-Saxon heir of Roman imperialism who, in the reign of Queen Elizabeth, had absolutely no possessions outside of Europe, has so outgrown his former limitations that he now shapes the courses of civilization in Asia, Africa, Australia, and portions of America by means of colonies, united, however, not by force, but by the ties of mutual interests and kindred blood which, consciously or unconsciously, are working ever toward the federation and amelioration of mankind.

THE THAMES, BELOW LONDON BRIDGE.

O silent, stately, and historic river, what suffering and sin hast thou not witnessed in thy ceaseless flow from Cæsar's century to our own! Would that thy waves had power either to cleanse the lives and consciences of men, or else, like fabled Lethe, to lift the awful load of London's misery and crime and bear it to an ocean of forgiveness and forgetfulness!

Conspicuous among the edifices of the "City" is a low-browed, massive structure, without a single window in its outer

NEARING THE SEA.

walls. It is the Bank of England. The absence of windows in its dark exterior is supposed to give greater security to its contents, the light within being obtained from interior courts and skylights. The building looks, therefore, like a gigantic strong box of granite, covering an area of four acres. Standing thus in the very heart of one of the busiest and most valuable localities in the world, this bank is suggestive of an electric power-house, — the central dynamo of the financial world. The sovereign here enthroned possesses a prerogative that no

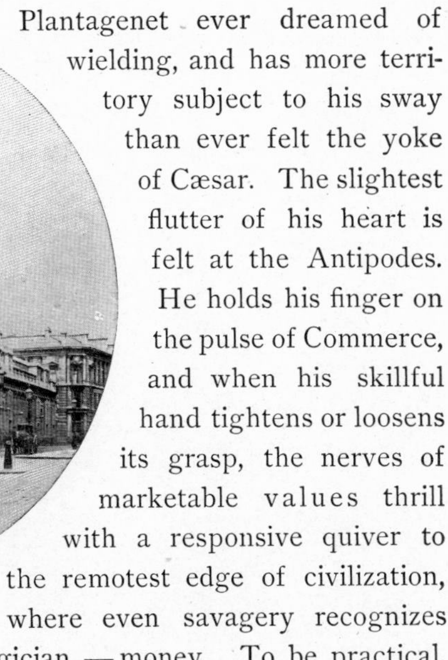

THE BANK OF ENGLAND.

Plantagenet ever dreamed of wielding, and has more territory subject to his sway than ever felt the yoke of Cæsar. The slightest flutter of his heart is felt at the Antipodes. He holds his finger on the pulse of Commerce, and when his skillful hand tightens or loosens its grasp, the nerves of marketable values thrill with a responsive quiver to the remotest edge of civilization, where even savagery recognizes now the influence of the magician, — money. To be practical, the capital of this bank is more than seventy-five millions of dollars, its private deposits aggregate double that amount, and its bullion is supposed to be worth at least one hundred and twenty-five millions. It determines the money-standard for every individual, and every transaction in an empire wider and more powerful

LUDGATE CIRCUS.

than that of Rome at her zenith; and, do what other countries may in rivalry, the Bank of England is the court of last appeal in all the world's financial differences. Yet this colossal institution is but two centuries old, born in the brain of a prophetic Scotchman, in 1694. Amsterdam, Venice, and a half dozen other European cities had banks before; but it remained for this child of William Patterson's invention to demonstrate the imperial dominion of which such an establishment is capable. I know of few things more suggestive than this enormous reservoir of monetary power. Great fortunes were accumulated under the older civilizations, but they were largely incidental, and never rose to be a dominating force. Riches were gained and wasted, then, without materially determining the rise and fall of nations. Our civilization, on the contrary, is guided and controlled by brain-force, wielding that mightiest of the brain's tools,—

STATUE OF GENERAL GORDON, TRAFALGAR SQUARE.

LAMBETH PALACE.

wealth. The great American authority on naval matters has demonstrated how necessary to supremacy is the mastery of the sea; but just as clearly does the history of the Bank of England prove that the possession of money predetermines that of naval power. It is now capital that gains control: first, of the highway of the world; and, secondly, of its commerce; and, hereafter, the ultimate victory in any war will depend upon the combatant's capacity to procure its "sinews." Hence, although grimy with soot and unimposing in architecture, the Bank of England is only less impressive to the thoughtful tourist than the Tower. One represents the power of the Present; the other illustrates the power of the Past. Before the coronation of Finance as King, there was no standard of political action save the caprice of individuals who governed "by divine right," and could make war at will; but with the rise of monetary power, and the enormous expense of modern ordnance (the firing of one shell costing thirteen hundred dollars), the undisputed sway of individual despots has forever passed away. The new régime is not without its possibilities of peril; yet it, at all events, has struck a death-blow to the former "one-man-power," and given to mankind another opportunity to help on the evolving freedom of the race.

HOTEL METROPOLE.

If the Place de la Concorde may be called the nucleus of Paris, that of London is Trafalgar Square. It will not do, however, to make too close a comparison between them, for in the neighborhood of the London square there is nothing approaching in impressiveness

TRAFALGAR SQUARE.

either the Garden of the Tuileries or the Champs Élysées. If the external charm of Paris may be likened to that of a beautiful, fascinating woman, that of London suggests a plain-featured and ill-dressed, but serious and intellectual, man. Nevertheless Trafalgar Square is not without attractions. The fluted granite column in the centre, flanked by the grand bronze lions of Sir Edwin Landseer, uplifts the colossal statue of the idol of the English, Admiral Nelson, who, in the glorious victory at Trafalgar, in 1805, destroyed the navy of the French and rendered futile Napoleon's audacious scheme of invading England. It is appro-

THE NELSON COLUMN.

priate that on the bronze reliefs of the pedestal, cast from the metal of French cannon, Nelson should be represented as declining, although fatally wounded, to be assisted by the surgeon before his turn; while one, also, reads there with moistened eyes the admiral's last command, immortalized by its simplicity and noble sentiment, "England expects every man to do his duty."

ADMIRAL NELSON.

Whoever comes to London expecting to find beautiful architecture will be woefully disappointed. Its parks are delightful, its pavements are probably the best in the world, and the display of luxury on such great thoroughfares as Regent and Oxford streets is most attractive; but, as a rule, the architecture of London is heavy and devoid of taste, while even the best of it is shrouded in an atmospheric drapery of diluted smut. Nor is this merely the impression of foreigners. No one could speak more severely of the ugliness of many of London's buildings than Englishmen themselves have done. Dickens has satirized them merci-

BASE OF THE NELSON COLUMN.

lessly, comparing some of them to tanks for holding fog; while of the National Gallery in Trafalgar Square an English writer has said: "This unhappy structure may be said to have everything it ought not to have, and nothing which it ought to have. It possesses windows without glass, a cupola without size, a portico without height, pepper boxes without pepper, and the finest site in Europe without anything to show upon it." Under such circumstances, a foreigner who first

THE DUKE OF WELLINGTON.

sees London on a raw November day is usually horribly depressed and thoroughly disenchanted, and might be tempted to imitate the German poet, Heine, who, on being taken to Westminster Abbey, the burial-place of famous Englishmen, handed the sexton a shilling, and said he would have given him more if the collection had been complete.

Even St. Paul's Cathedral usually disappoints the visitor. The exterior is, indeed, imposing, and the great dome is like

THE IMPERIAL INSTITUTE, SOUTH KENSINGTON.

a temple in the air, three hundred and sixty-five feet above the street, and one hundred and forty-five in diameter. It is, however, so black with the grimy incense that innumerable chimneys have been offering up to it for two hundred years, that a Frenchman suggested that it must have been built by chimney-sweeps! It is a curious fact that the total cost of this cathedral was defrayed by a tax on every ton of coal brought to the port of London; so that, after all, no building in the world is better entitled to a sooty exterior. What has impressed me most in St. Paul's is its comparative isolation, even though standing in the great throbbing heart of London. It is, in fact, so lofty that it seems wholly unaffected by its environment. Despite the roar and tumult nothing disturbs its grand serenity. We are reminded of the words of Goethe:

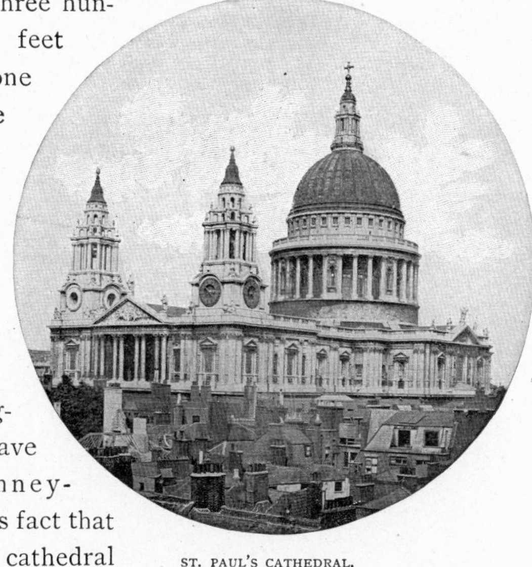

ST. PAUL'S CATHEDRAL.

THE ENTRANCE TO ST. PAUL'S.

"On every height there lies repose."

Another singular fact in the history of this church is that the first stone which the architect ordered the masons to bring from the rubbish of the former cathedral, destroyed by fire, was part of a sarcophagus, on which had been inscribed the single word, "*Resurgam*,"—"I shall rise again." The prophecy was fulfilled, and for its resurrection in its present form the world is indebted to Sir Christopher Wren, who sleeps, within the temple that he reared, under the epitaph, "If you seek his monument, look around you."

THE INTERIOR OF ST. PAUL'S.

It must be said of the interior of St. Paul's that it is bare and cheerless. Although gigantic, it awakens no enthusiasm, especially if one is familiar with cathedrals on the Continent, whose walls and columns gleam with polished marble, whose pavements are of beautiful mosaic, and whose stained glass portrays the lives of saints in glowing colors. But here the walls are bare, the windows colorless, the arches empty as a hollow skull; the columns show the plain stone blocks, and even the cement that holds them; while the vast dome, which might be rendered glorious with mosaics, looks like a huge receptacle for fog and dust. Most of the statues in St. Paul's are, also, in deplorably bad taste, and some of them are positively ludicrous. Old Doctor Johnson, for example, is represented by a half-nude figure, suggestive of an athlete catching cold. We all know that the author of the Dictionary was negligent in dress, but why he should have been portrayed almost entirely deprived of clothing is a mystery. Still more objectionable is the statue of a Captain Burgess, who stands entirely nude, as he receives a sword from the Goddess of Victory. Two admirals have, also, unclothed statues, which strikes one as absurd, since nudity has never been the uniform of British officers, even in India.

THE NAVE OF ST. PAUL'S.

ST. PAUL'S, FROM THE RIVER.

I have tried to speak with absolute impartiality of London. It is in some respects the most interesting, and in others the most uninteresting, city of the modern world. The tourist should cherish no illusions in regard to some of its material features. Its fog, which Hawthorne calls "the spiritual medium of departed mud," its usually unattractive architecture, its hideous coverlet of soot, its indescribably dismal Sundays, its endless gin-shops, from which gray-haired women often reel intoxicated, its conservative hotel methods and unappetizing

WESTMINSTER BRIDGE-ROAD.

cuisine, often cause London to appear, at first, a place from which to flee as soon as possible. But, presently, the other side reveals itself, and we begin to admire its perfectly paved streets, its low-priced cabs, its admirable municipal government, its wonderful museums, its priceless literary and historic memories, its exhibitions of everything artistic and remarkable that human genius can produce, and, above all, its spacious parks. It gives one an idea not only of the immensity of London as a whole, but, also, of the vastness of its "breathing places," to learn that, almost in the centre of the city, he can start at the northwest corner of Kensington Gardens and walk over green grass for four and a half miles. Moreover, a very practical source of pleasure in London is the prompt and intelligent service rendered by subordinates. Grant that a "tip" is universally expected for the favor; it is a pleasure to reward good service, and London is not the only city in the world where fees make life run smoothly.

HYDE PARK.

But though the greater part of London's architecture be commonplace or positively ugly, the influence of history awakens interest where art has failed, and many a locality, which would be otherwise merely dingy and prosaic, attracts us irresistibly as the

ROTTEN ROW.

abode of some imaginary character of fiction, and holds us spellbound by the subtile power of the master's thought. The catalogue of literary stars that have blazed forth upon the London firmament, even in the present century, is well-nigh endless: Carlyle, the rugged cynic; Bulwer, the polished man of society; Disraeli, that curious blending of the romancer and statesman; George Eliot, the most gifted of modern women; Dickens, the unsurpassed interpreter of humble life; Thackeray, the keen but kindly satirist, — all these have breathed a spirit of humanity into these old walls and set the stamp of genius upon its stones; and, as the men illustrious in Greek letters were indissolubly linked with Athens, so in the list of English authors there is scarcely a name that is not interwoven with the history of London.

DICKENS' HOUSE, DEVONSHIRE TERRACE.

None of these writers, however, is so closely identified with this city by the Thames as Dickens, who found its streets at

THE PROMENADE, HYDE PARK.

once his workshop, and the principal source of his inspiration. It was from London's street signs that he usually gleaned the names peculiar to his characters; and he kept a book, in which he noted down the odd names that in his daily walks attracted his attention. Subsequently he would combine the first syllable of one with the last syllable of another, producing, as we know, the most extraordinary results. The names he finally selected were commonly the survival of the fittest, and many a now familiar title has passed in Dickens' mind through several changes. Thus, "Martin Chuzzlewit" was the ultimate choice out of Martin Sweezleden, Sweezlewag, Chuzzletoe, Chuzzleboy, Chubblewig, and half a dozen more.

DOUGHTY STREET.

Lovers of Dickens can easily drive to his different London residences, the principal ones being Furnival's Inn, Devonshire Terrace, Tavistock Square, and Doughty Street. It was

GOLDEN CROSS HOTEL.

while living in the last-mentioned place that Dickens laid the stepping-stones to his unprecedented popularity, by writing the "Pickwick Papers," the sale of which at one bound far outstripped that of any other book within the century. It fascinated everybody, high and low, from solemn judges on the bench to laughing boys in the street, and its humor, like the piper's music, made all people dance, whether they would or not.

Carlyle tells of a clergyman, who, having ended his exhortation to a sick parishioner, was leaving the room when he heard the sick man murmur something. The minister paused, hoping to catch some echo of his solemn utterances. What was his surprise to hear the invalid exclaim, "Well, thank God, Pickwick will be out in ten days, anyhow!"

In fact, only space is wanting to enumerate the many spots in London identified, beyond a reasonable doubt, as those which figure in the works of Dickens, and to which of late years several books have been devoted. With these as guides, the tourist can easily prepare a list, and, at his leisure, drive or walk to every place that he desires to see; whether it be the Golden Cross Hotel, where Steerforth lodged, and in front of which Mr. Pickwick had his encounter with a cabby; or St.

Andrew's Church, which Oliver Twist and Bill Sikes passed on their way to commit a burglary; or Newgate Prison, where Fagin waited for his doom; or Ralph Nickleby's house, in Golden Square; or the Crown Inn, where Mr. Newman Noggs was known; or Mantelini's dress-making establishment, in Wigmore Street; or Kingsgate Street, the home of Sairey Gamp. Moreover, in one of London's busiest thoroughfares, we may still read the sign of "Dombey & Son"; another structure bears the name of the "Old Curiosity Shop"; and we may eat a chop in the George & Vulture Tavern, with its souvenirs of Sam Weller; or, almost in the shadow of St. Paul's, see Bevis Marks, which, thanks to Dickens' wit, has echoed to the laughter of the world. For here, "in a small dark house, so near the sidewalk that the parlor windows were only cleaned by the elbows of the passers-by," lived the impecunious Dick Swiveller; Miss Sally Brass, "whose sallow complexion was only relieved by the healthy glow on the tip of her nose"; and the half-starved Marchioness, who was fed in the cellar-kitchen, where everything was padlocked, including the grate, and where there was not enough food left out for even a beetle to lunch on.

Those who desire to trace the scenes of "Little Dorrit" can easily verify the words of Dickens: "Whoever turns from Angel Court into Marshalsea Palace will find his feet upon the pave-

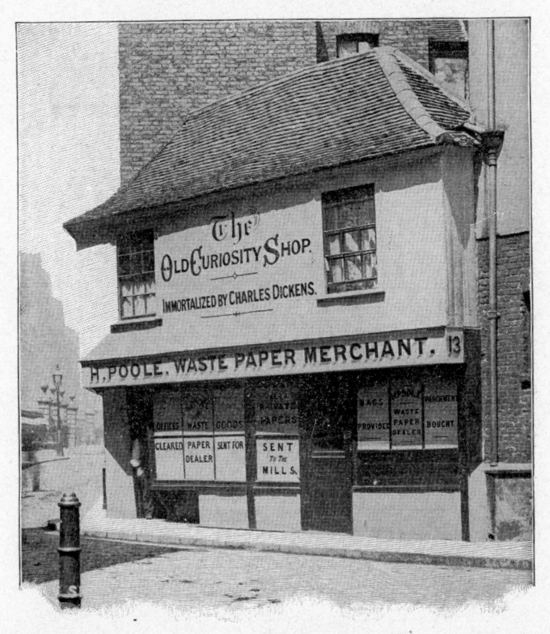

THE "OLD CURIOSITY SHOP."

ment of the prison; will find the courtyard very little altered, if at all; will see the debtors' rooms, and stand among the crowding ghosts of many miserable years." Obeying these instructions, I found indeed the courtyard; but it has somewhat changed since Dickens' time. It is no longer a debtors' jail, but is connected with another form of human misery, being a cheap lodging-house for some of the poorest of the London poor. Yet an officer pointed out to me the room where Arthur Clennam passed the night, when accidentally locked in; and the old pump, which Dickens describes as marking the aristocratic side of the yard, where Mr. Dorrit always walked, as "The Father of the Marshalsea"; and I even climbed two flights of stairs to see some shabby rooms, ascribed by Dickens to Mr. Dorrit and his faithful child, and which really formed once the abode of Mr. and Mrs. Dickens, and were visited, alas! only too often by the novelist when a boy. One who wishes to study the localities mentioned in "Bleak House" can easily make his way to "No. 58," Lincoln's Inn, a spacious mansion, which Dickens no doubt had in mind

A PART OF THE MARSHALSEA PRISON.

LODGE IN ST. JAMES' PARK.

when he described the residence of the secretive old lawyer, Mr. Tulkinghorn, whom he called "an oyster of the old school whom nobody could open." The novelist was perfectly familiar with the building, since it was here that his friend and biographer, Forster, lived; and here, one winter's night, Dickens, who had just come from Italy to superintend the publication of his new Christmas story, "The Chimes," read it to Forster, Carlyle, Jerrold, and other friends. Maclise, the artist, made a sketch of the party, and in it one can see the frescos on the ceiling which Dickens often speaks of in "Bleak House," —weird figures with waving arms and ghostly fingers, forever pointing at the fatal spot where Tulkinghorn was destined to lie, face downward on the floor, shot through the heart!

KINGSGATE STREET
(RESIDENCE OF SAIREY GAMP).

A still more pathetic memorial of "Bleak House" is the pauper's burial-ground, whither Jo conducted Lady Dedlock, disguised as a servant, that she might look upon the wretched ending of a life which Love had once knit closely to her own. So dark is the dismal alley leading to this fearful place that, when I brought a photographer to the place, we were obliged to bribe the custodian to open the gate, in order to obtain light enough to render visible the steps, where at last poor Lady Dedlock, a fugitive from her home, came to die near the grave of the man she had loved.

One of the richest monuments, not only of London, but of the whole world, is the celebrated Albert Memorial, — a structure erected to the memory of the husband of Queen Victoria. The pedestal alone repays an hour of close inspection. Broad granite steps lead up on every side to a spacious platform, at the corners of which are four colossal groups of statuary, symbolic of the great divisions of the globe: Europe, Asia, Africa, and America. Beyond these, the base of the tower, which rises from the centre of the platform, is nothing less than wonderful in its elaborate display of one hundred and sixty-nine life-sized marble statues cut in high relief, and surrounding the entire monument. These noble forms portray the greatest geniuses of every period since the dawn of history: painters, sculptors, musicians, architects, inventors, reformers, poets, and philosophers. In one place, for example, stands

THE ALBERT MEMORIAL.

Homer, the "Father of Poetry," while near him, reverentially listening to his words, are Virgil, Dante, Shakespeare, Cervantes, Milton, and Boccaccio. In another section are grouped Michelangelo, Donatello, Ghiberti, John of Bologna, Benvenuto Cellini, and other sculptors of the Renaissance. At last, above them all, rises to the height of one hundred and seventy-five feet a gorgeously decorated Gothic spire, glittering with gilding, sparkling with multicolored mosaics, crowded with

THE RELIEFS.

HOMER AND HIS SUCCESSORS.

EUROPE.

bronze and marble statues of angels blowing golden trumpets, and, finally, surmounted by a golden cross; while under this magnificent canopy, which is almost Oriental in the splendor of its decoration, sits a statue of gilded bronze fifteen feet in height, portraying the Prince Consort.

To one who did not know the high esteem felt for Prince Albert, by the people of Great Britain, it might seem strange that such a magnificent memorial should be erected to a German prince, who had derived his chief political distinction by marrying Queen Victoria. But, when one calls to mind the enormous influence for good or ill that any husband can exert over a wife, who loves him and is the mother of his

AMERICA.

children, one can appreciate the immense relief and gratitude awakened in all English hearts, when it became evident that the Prince Consort's influence with the Queen was not only personally great and good, but in affairs of State was also al-

ASIA.

ways exerted for the welfare of the land she ruled. More than to any other Englishman, save John Bright, America (as well as England) is deeply indebted to Prince Albert, for having sturdily and steadfastly upheld the cause of the Union in our Civil War; and it was on his arm that the Queen leaned, with confident reliance, during that period, so momentous for the two great divisions of the English-speaking race.

AFRICA.

A perfect gentleman, a man of irreproachable character, a loving husband, a wise and devoted father, an earnest patron of art and science, and the promoter of the first of the World's Great Expositions, Great Britain has done well to honor, worthily, the Consort of its Sovereign and the father of its future king.

VICTORIA TOWER.

The best view of England's Houses of Parliament is obtained from the river along which they extend for nearly one thousand feet. Built in elaborate Gothic style, their ornamentation includes massive towers, graceful pinnacles, fluted columns, interesting statues, and a bewildering amount of fine stone-carving. They cover an area of eight acres; and while their rooms are numbered by hundreds, their corridors can be reckoned by miles.

The grand Victoria Tower, through which the Queen enters when she opens Parliament, attains the imposing height of three hundred and forty feet. The Clock Tower, also, at the northern end of these imperial legislative halls, is only twenty feet lower than its rival. It gives one a singular conception of force producing delicate results when he learns that the minute-hand on that lofty clock-dial is a bar of steel twelve feet in length. Every one, who has spent a night in this part of London, must have heard the great bell of this tower proclaim the flight of time in deep and solemn tones, which are to those of other bells like the diapason of an organ to the sound of a street piano. This bell, which weighs no less than thirteen tons, is called Big Ben, and had for years no rival; but it is now surpassed by the monster recently placed in St. Paul's Cathedral; yet they are far enough apart to cause no interference with each other. The kingdom of Big Ben has been curtailed, but over this part of gigantic London he still reigns supreme.

CLOCK TOWER.

The hall where the Peers of England sit in council is sumptuously decorated. The stained glass windows glow with the illumined forms of all the kings and queens of England since the Conquest; around the walls, on gilded pillars, stand statues of the valiant barons who forced Magna Charta from King John; while the rich filigree and carving on al-

THE ENTRANCE TO THE HOUSE OF LORDS.

most every foot of wall and balcony make the apartment seem a trifle overladen with adornment. In the centre stands the famous wool-sack of the Lord Chancellor, a kind of cushioned ottoman, covered with crimson cloth; while on the right and left are the seats of the Lords, who do not occupy chairs and desks, as do our Senators, but long benches upholstered in leather.

At one end of the hall, beneath a richly gilded canopy, stands the throne of the Queen; and the two Houses are so

THE HOUSE OF LORDS.

arranged that when the doors are opened, her Majesty, seated in the House of Lords, can see in a direct line the Speaker of the House of Commons in his chair.

To Englishmen and Americans who have been present at debates in the House of Commons during the latter half of the nineteenth century, three Parliamentary heroes stand forth unsurpassed in interest and influence. They are John Bright, the sturdy champion of the Union during the Civil War in the United States; Benjamin Disraeli, the brilliant leader of the Tories; and William E. Gladstone, whom even contemporaneous history designated by the title, Grand Old Man.

HOUSES OF PARLIAMENT, FROM THE THAMES.

THE THRONE.

It was never my privilege to listen to John Bright, but I have more than once sat spellbound under the sonorous voice and rhythmic eloquence of Gladstone, and have followed with intense enthusiasm forensic struggles between the sinuous Disraeli and his sturdy foe. For years, on every important question, either Disraeli spoke first and Gladstone answered him, or Gladstone advocated the measure and was replied to by his rival. The contrast between these men, whom politics made lifelong parliamentary adversaries, was striking; yet one could scarcely doubt for a moment which was the greater statesman, orator, and scholar. Glad-

THE HOUSE OF COMMONS.

JOHN BRIGHT.

stone was always perfectly sincere. He spoke with the assurance of conviction and the courageous confidence of an approving conscience. Disraeli, on the contrary, never appeared to believe thoroughly a word he said, but seemed to take a gamester's view of life, and to be half cynically, half wearily, pushing about kings, queens, knights, pawns, and bishops upon the chess-board of the world.

The face of Gladstone beamed with animation, sparkled with intelligence, glowed with fervor, and merited what Justin McCarthy said of it, that it was the most magnificent human face he ever saw. Disraeli's countenance, however, was as inscrutable as that of the Sphinx. Oriental in imagery, fertile of invention, rich in ridicule, master of invective, and the sovereign of sarcasm, he made replies to Gladstone which at times reminded me of the keen thrust of the matador to the charging bull; and some of his superlatively stinging phrases, as when he described his great opponent as "inebriated with his own

BENJAMIN DISRAELI.

verbosity," and as "a man without one redeeming fault," cut into a controversy like vitriol into human flesh. But, after all, no thoughtful and unprejudiced auditor could leave the House of Commons after such a duel in debate without a recognition of the Liberal's superiority.

Both of these leaders have now passed away. The thrilling, penetrating, and melodious tones which carried Gladstone's noble periods to his hearers, as the great trade winds sweep on full-sailed ships to their desired havens, are now hushed forever; and the low, vibrant voice of Beaconsfield, cutting the eager stillness of the rapt House, like the sword of Saladin, has likewise passed into the silence of the tomb. But none who ever heard them can forget them; and as he looks upon the places which those men once occupied when they in turn were Premiers of England, no other figures will suggest themselves so readily to his memory and imagination as those of the great Hebrew novelist, who gave to Queen Victoria the title Empress of India, and the grand orator, statesman, scholar, theologian, linguist, and literary critic, William Ewart Gladstone.

MR. GLADSTONE.

Strangely enough, this dwelling-place of the real power of the British Empire occupies the identical ground where, in the days when England's sovereign could say, with almost as much truth as Louis XIV., "I am the State," stood an abode of royalty. Accordingly, this memorable site, which was the home of kings, is now the home of the British people, as represented in the persons of those chosen for their lawmakers.

The Parliament of Great Britain is not a gift, but a growth; not a boon granted by a generous ruler, but a development by the people, often unconscious of their work, and building better than they knew. Nor was it the invention of one individual, or of a conference deliberately appointed for the task. Its seed, apparently congenital with the Anglo-Saxon race, germinated as far back as the thirteenth century, and bore its first fruit in Magna Charta.

THE PRINCES' CHAMBER.

Standing on this historic site, it is a suggestive thought to an American or Englishman that only the Anglo-Saxon has succeeded in giving to the idea of democracy permanent growth. The Greeks and Romans founded what they called "republics"; but they were, really, nothing more than oligarchies; and when the dwellers by the Tiber rose, at last, against the steadily increasing power of a ruling class, it was too late; for out of popular disorders had arisen Imperialism, which, though it reigned for centuries in splendor, was a distinctively backward step, and ended, finally, in ruin. More than a thousand years later, the mad revolt of the French people revived the democratic idea, but they soon drowned

THE FOREIGN OFFICE.

it in their own best blood, and mankind saw another Latin race slide backward into Cæsarism. In the political evolution of the Anglo-Saxon, however, there has been no serious retrogression in the evolution of democracy. Far back in primitive Saxon days the whole tribe held a General Meeting to declare its will. A little later came the Council of the Wise Men, which marked a distinct advance beyond the general tribal gathering, and was the unsuspected embryo of the present system of representation. Still later, the political genius that had planned this for a single tribe, made the arrangement *intertribal*, and in coöperative action against outside foes furnished the germ of the modern idea of national federation. At present both England and America are really working toward the same ends on parallel lines; and since the separation of mother and child, in 1776, Great Britain has been developing the democratic idea almost as rapidly as the United States. Perhaps the greater reverence felt by Englishmen for conservative forms has kept the elder nation from a few extreme ideas that we shall yet discard, and, possibly, we may hereafter view with more appreciation the splendidly progressive yet conservative way in which Great Britain has

HAMPDEN.

BURKE.

KING EDWARD VII.

contrived to build the ever-broadening power of the people, without, however, trampling under foot some precious privileges born from the antecedent travail of mankind.

For more than five hundred years a constant struggle has been going on in the Anglo-Saxon race between the idea of absolute kingship and that of popular participation in political power. The former has been steadily losing ground, while the path of the latter has been continually widening, till now the real Government of the United Kingdom is lodged in the House of Commons. The almost absolute Elizabeth, of three hundred years ago, would have regarded the political condition which exists in England now, as the annihilation of the royal prerogative; yet never under Elizabeth, or any other English sovereign, did British royalty, which has to-day for its high exponent Queen Victoria, stand on a foundation so embellished by affection, hallowed by reverence, and buttressed by loyalty.

QUEEN ALEXANDRA.

To the thoughtful tourist in London, the object of greatest interest is Westminster Abbey. Prayers have ascended from its consecrated site for nearly

MARLBOROUGH HOUSE.

thirteen hundred years, and parts of even the present structure date from 1065. Moreover, after the bareness of St. Paul's, it is with genuine delight that we walk through the pillared aisles of this old Gothic Pile, whose pointed arches, fluted columns, and immense rose windows, which fill the temple with a softened light and bring a flush of color to the time-stained walls, are all in harmony with the inspiring thoughts suggested by the hallowed shrine. It is, however, neither its age nor architectural impressiveness that gives greatest glory to this edifice. Westminster Abbey is England's Pantheon of Genius. There is no Temple of Fame in the whole world to equal it. The Church of Santa Croce, at Florence, most nearly resembles it; yet the illustrious Italians buried there are but a handful to the mighty dead who slumber in this temple by the Thames; and the Walhalla of the Germans, at Regensburg, above the Danube, although magnificent, is not a burial-place, while all its monuments are modern and its associations purely secular. But England's minster wears the triple crown of noble architecture, venerable age, and hallowed memories, and through each aisle and chapel of this national mausoleum flows the majestic stream of English history, none the less real because invisible.

WESTMINSTER ABBEY.

THE TOWERS OF THE ABBEY.

It will be easily comprehended, therefore, that to try to explore thoroughly this city of the dead at a single visit, is as unwise as to inspect with equal brevity the Vatican, or the Louvre. The tourist who attempts so profitless a task irreparably wrongs himself, by weakening, or forever losing, the ennobling thoughts which cannot be awakened in the mind of one who is exhausted or confused. Westminster Abbey should be visited repeatedly, for about an hour at a time: once, for example, to note only its ancient monuments; a second time,

THE CHOIR.

TOMB OF HENRY III.

to see the graves and cenotaphs of its more recent dead; and, later still, to enjoy the general architectural effect of the whole edifice; while there can be no limit to the number of occasions when one may profitably leave the noisy streets and spend an hour in the sacred silence of the Poets' Corner. He must be singularly irresponsive to impressions who can look, unmoved, upon the tombs and effigies of England's kings and queens, whose history is also ours, and think how little is the area that now constitutes their empire! Some of these royal statues lie outstretched upon their tombs, while others kneel in prayer; but all of them alike — conquerors and conquered, friends and foes, murderers and their victims — lie silent and at peace, at last, within the solemn shadow of the Abbey's roof. Yet these sculptured sovereigns have not remained entirely unmolested. Some of their graves have been disturbed. The tomb

TOMB OF EDWARD III.

THE TOMB OF QUEEN ELIZABETH.

of Edward the Confessor was once broken open by some human ghoul, and even the marble figure of Elizabeth no longer wears its golden crown. How can she rest here now so quietly when only a chapel's width divides her from her rival, Mary, Queen of Scots? Did they both carry their hostility beyond the grave? Have they met? What are now their relative positions? In vain we lose ourselves in such conjectures, for though we ask to-day the same sad questions uttered by the patriarch Job, and the Persian Omar, we find no adequate reply.

THE CORONATION CHAIR.

Surrounded by these royal tombs, stands one of the most interesting relics of antiquity to be found in any land. It is the celebrated Stone of Destiny on which the kings of Scotland had been crowned for centuries before it came into the possession of the English. Legend declares that it was the pillow on which the Hebrew patriarch, Jacob, laid his head when he beheld the vision of the celestial ladder; tradition, also, affirms that, before its advent into Scotland, it rested upon the Sacred Hill of Tara and formed the coronation seat of Irish kings; thence it was taken to the island of Iona, and it is possible that on this block of old red sandstone lay the head of St. Columba as he breathed his last upon that sacred isle. But it is certain that King Edward I. of England, in 1297, brought this coronation stone from Scotland and placed it in Westminster Abbey, ordering that it should be encased in a chair of oak. This was done, and it thrills one to remember, as he looks on this memorial of the past, that to all the previous associations connected with it has been added this: that in the chair enclosing it all of England's sovereigns have been crowned for the last six hundred years.

THE JENNY LIND TABLET.

In recent years the burials in the Abbey have been marked with far less ostentatious monuments than formerly. Some who repose here have no monuments; but in the pavement, on the marble slabs that hide their precious dust, we merely read their names. It is noticeable, too, that lengthy epitaphs are now usually omitted. Whether this is always a gain depends upon the taste of the composer. Thus, the inscription on the tomb of the poet Gay is utterly unsuited to the solemn features of the Abbey:

"Life is a jest, and all things show it;
I thought so once, but now I know it."

While, on the other hand, one of the most beautiful and appropriate epitaphs I have ever read adorns the monument to the Arctic explorer, Sir John Franklin, who perished in the frozen North. Its concluding words are these: "This monument was erected by his widow, who, after long waiting and sending many in search of him, herself departed to seek and find him in the realms of light."

SIR JOHN FRANKLIN'S MONUMENT.

It is only after a visit to Westminster that we can thoroughly appreciate the words of Dean Stanley, uttered just before his death: "As far as I understood what the duties of my office were supposed to be, in spite of every incompetence, I am yet humbly trustful that I have sustained before the mind of the nation the extraordinary value of the Abbey as a religious, national, and liberal institution." Extraordinary, indeed, seems

THE NATIONAL TREASURY.

THE TOMB OF DEAN STANLEY.

the value of this edifice as we walk thoughtfully along what is known as the Aisle of Statesmen, and look upon the busts or statues of such men as Robert Peel, Lord Palmerston, William Pitt, Grattan, Canning, Fox, and Benjamin Disraeli, Earl of Beaconsfield; and it must be inspiring to an Englishman to tread this storied pavement and realize what a heritage of undying glory has come down to him under their guidance in the slow,

THE AVENUE OF STATESMEN.

LORD PALMERSTON.

steady progress of the parliamentary principle. Now that the dust of the arena has cleared, the impartial critic sees that all those forensic gladiators, though at times mistaken, profited sooner or later by the lessons of experience; and, while considering first the glory of their own country, yet, in their recognition of that country's duties toward humanity, used their commanding oratory and constructive statesmanship for the development of a loftier standard of ideals and the diffusion of a higher civilization.

Nor are the forms of heroes and philanthropists wanting here. We look, for example, on memorials of Colin Campbell, who recaptured Lucknow; Sir James Outram, the "Bayard of India"; Livingstone, the African explorer; and Sir James Simpson, who, by his discovery of chloroform as

TOMB OF DAVID LIVINGSTONE.

an anæsthetic, has relieved incalculable suffering in the human race. Not far from these, Sir Charles Lyell, the distinguished geologist; Sir John Herschel, the eminent astronomer; Charles Darwin, the great naturalist; and Sir Isaac Newton, the philosopher, all lie within a few yards of one another.

But specially beautiful — both in its architecture and in the colored light which wraps the tombs and statues in a robe of glory — the Poets' Corner of Westminster Abbey seems the

THE POETS' CORNER.

ideal resting-place of those rare souls selected by the Muses to be their interpreters. It is not strange that this part of the Abbey appeals to us more than any other, for every footstep on its marble pavement falls upon a grave, and its gray walls are lined with tablets, busts, and monuments containing names which have become to us household words. Great conquerors, wise ecclesiastics, and even gifted statesmen do not touch our hearts as do the poets and authors whose works are in our

CHAUCER'S TOMB.

libraries, and whom, in many an hour by our firesides, we have learned to love and reverence as friends. Thus, close by the marble tomb of Chaucer, and hence associated with that "Father of English Poetry" over an interval of five hundred years, lie Robert Browning, and Alfred Tennyson; while, in proof of the kinship of all writers in our glorious Anglo-Saxon tongue, we see not far from these the kindly face of Henry Wadsworth Longfellow. Here, too, upon the wall is the bust of Shakespeare's friend and fellow-poet, "O rare Ben Jonson"; and within its shadow is the grave of Edmund Spenser, who, though he died in misery, yet had

MEMORIALS OF A GROUP OF POETS.

a funeral here which kings might envy but could not obtain; for Beaumont, Fletcher, Ben Jonson, and probably Shakespeare attended it; and poems written by these men of genius, together with the pens that had inscribed them, were thrown into Spenser's open grave. Although the author of the

SHAKESPEARE.

"Elegy in a Country Churchyard" "rests his head upon the lap of earth," in the rustic cemetery of Stoke Pogis, a beautiful medallion of his face, beneath the bust of Milton, here "invokes the passing tribute of a sigh." Immortal Shakespeare, too, supreme and unapproachable, looks calmly down upon the tombs of his successors, and wonderfully solemn and impressive seem his lines from the "Tempest," carved on the scroll within his hand:

> "The cloud-capp'd towers, the gorgeous palaces,
> The solemn temples, the great globe itself,
> Yea, all which it inherit, shall dissolve
> And, like this insubstantial pageant faded,
> Leave not a rack behind."

Here, also, we see the burial-place of David Garrick, the actor, whose death was said to have eclipsed the gaiety of nations, and at whose funeral Burke remarked that Shakespeare's statue seemed to be pointing to the grave where the great interpreter of his works was laid. Not far away is the tomb of the composer Händel, whose funeral was attended by three thousand people; and near him the marble bust of Thackeray looks on the grave of his great contemporary Dickens. It is, however, impossible to enumerate all of England's sons of genius who are represented here: Southey, Campbell, Coleridge, Thomson, Burns, Goldsmith, Dryden, Addison, greatest of English essayists; Samuel Johnson, the lexicographer; Bulwer Lytton, the novelist; Sheridan, the dramatist; and Macaulay, the historian and poet, — the pure white features of all these relieve the shadows of Westminster, as their immortal works give light and beauty to the world. And what a literature is

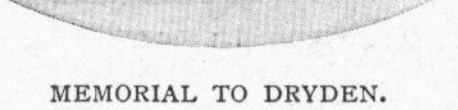

MEMORIAL TO DRYDEN.

that whose representatives slumber in this Necropolis of Genius! There is not a theme in history, poetry, science, romance, or philosophy that it has not touched upon, illumined, and embellished. Next to the literature of

GRAVE OF BULWER LYTTON.

Greece, it is at once the most voluminous and luminous the world has ever known, and all the forms in which reflection, reason, and imagination have attempted to reveal themselves have found expression in its works of genius. However great the debt which mankind owes the English-speaking race for fostering and developing political liberty, far greater is its claim to human gratitude

WHERE TENNYSON LIES BURIED.

for opening the entire field of reason to investigation, and leveling every barrier to debate. The highest glory of the Anglo-Saxon comes from the fact that he has made himself the champion of intellectual freedom, and has, for centuries, asserted and maintained man's privilege to speak and write his thought.

ENGLAND'S GUARDSMEN.